D1527852

FAITH, FOCUS AND LEADERSHIP

Keys to Excellence in Six Episcopal Churches

Peter A. R. Stebinger

Peter A. R. Stebinger is rector of Christ Episcopal Church, Bethany, Connecticut. This book grew out of a sabbatical project in 1988. Publication was made possible by a grant from the Church Missions Publishing Company.

CONTENTS

the use of physical and financial resources: St. George's, York Harbor, Maine...

4

What is excellence?

It is currently fashionable to declare that the Episcopal Church is dying. Few people can be found who will say that the church is vibrant and alive except in a few "megachurches," parishes good at letting their light shine. Yet there are many excellent parishes in the Episcopal Church. This book is the result of a study of six of them.

The six vary in size, from 33 to 680 members; budget, from $26,500 to $289,000; style, from staid traditional to exuberant liberal; and location, South Carolina to Maine. Few people, myself included, believed when the study began that these parishes would share any common characteristics. Yet the study revealed extraordinary similarities; areas of common practice so consistent that I believe that they may apply to 90 per cent of the Episcopal churches in this country.

The study reveals three constants.

First, the basics of the faith are taught and lived out in each church community in much the same way. The faith is taught primarily through preaching by the clergy of short, one point, biblically-based, personally relevant sermons which cause people to reflect on their daily lives and which reveal the presence of God to them in the midst of the ordinary. The faith is lived out through the exemplary life of the clergy and also through the efforts of members of the congregation to live the Christian life as best they can through service to one another and to the world.

Second, each parish or mission has a primary focus for the common life of their community. This may be local mission work. It may be mutual support and fellowship given primarily to one another. It may be the sharing of the good news of the gospel with others. In each community a *single* primary focus is present, sometimes subtle, sometimes obvious, but it is there.

Third, each congregation is led by a highly skilled priest who provides the key leadership. This leadership is strong, clear and has as one of its highest values the strengthening of the local community of faith. It is leadership which seeks consensus yet can take a stand if needed. It is leadership which allows disagreement and is skilled at conflict management, by training or by intuition. It is leadership which is powerful but not autocratic. Strong clerical leadership has led to strong lay leadership and high levels of lay involvement.

Much of the rest of this book will be devoted to a detailed description of the six churches. But first, we look at the process by which they were selected.

6

Early in January, 1988, after the setting up of a research design with the help of Dr. Jackson Carroll of the Hartford Seminary Foundation, the next step was choosing research sites. The best data would be generated if the study parishes were very different from one another, having excellence as their only common characteristic. The national Episcopal Church was asked to name bishops and diocesan staff in the South and Northeast who knew well the parishes within their dioceses. These persons would be in a good position to select subjects for this study. The Diocese of South Carolina and the Diocese of Maine were selected from a larger list provided by Dr. Arlin Rothage, a staff officer in parish development at the national church.

The four people who made the parish selections were the Rt. Rev. C. FitzSimmons Allison, Bishop of South Carolina; the Venerable Jack Beckwith, Archdeacon of South Carolina; the Rt. Rev. Edward Chalfant, Bishop of Maine, and Mr. Hank Hancock, Canon to the Ordinary of Maine. Archdeacon Beckwith and Canon Hancock were the staff people primarily responsible for congregations within their diocesan structures. The four were asked to select two excellent parishes in each of three size categories, and later were interviewed about their selection criteria. These interviews revealed many areas

7

of common agreement.

Some of the criteria for excellence are measurable. All four looked for an increased strength in stewardship. There should be more dollars available to support the parish budget year after year and the amount contributed by each giving unit should be increasing. There should be an increase in activity by the people of the parish and few problems recruiting people for its work.

The excellent parish will do better than its surrounding community in the change of the number of members and the number of people who attend worship. This is important. For most parishes serving areas with population growth this will mean increase rates greater than the region's. But some excellent parishes serve areas in which the population is decreasing or stable. In these parishes a constant or slightly increasing number of people on the rolls and at worship can be a sign of excellence.

All excellent parishes will have an increase in the percentage of income devoted to outreach and in the amount of activity devoted to reaching out into the community at large. The nature of these activities can vary.

Along with these measurable criteria a number of "softer" indicators of excellence emerged.

A strong commitment to deepening the

8

spiritual life of people of the parish was cited by all. Most often the crucial causes of spiritual deepening were strong preaching of the gospel and working with people to deepen their relationship with God. Evidence supporting this belief was gathered through reading parish bulletins and talking with the people during parish visits.

A strong commitment to lay leadership and support of the ministry of the laity was cited as another criteria. Are the laity involved in all aspects of parish life? Do they have a part in key decisions? Are they supported by the clergy?

The bishops and staff looked for worship which is welcoming and joyful. Is the parish filled with energy on Sunday morning? Would a person want to come back to church? Do you feel uplifted after participating in a service?

Bishop Chalfant cited one final criteria that I believe would be supported by all four. Would anyone outside the church know or care if this parish disappeared? This question points to the impact of the church on the community in which it is situated.

All of the parishes in this study fit these criteria.

THE PARISHES

The next chapter will look at the "whys" of

excellence. Two pieces of background information will be helpful in that discussion: first, descriptions of the parishes studied, and second the method of data collection.

The parish called Christ Church in Peachtree, South Carolina is the only one whose rector asked for anonymity. So the town, his name and the name of the parish have been changed. He did not want people to "think I have gotten a big head." The rector, the Rev. Dr. John Frost, has been there for over 23 years.

The town of Peachtree is an old southern community. Its buildings are now aging and the economy has shifted from being based in agriculture to being rooted in manufacturing and the service sector. The city has roughly doubled in size over the last twenty years to a population of 15,500 in 1984. Its downtown is rundown and most of the better shops are now located in a regional mall about six miles out of town. It is, in short, a "typical" southern community.

Christ Church is a complex of buildings which have grown up over the years. The church was begun in 1848 as a square building seating about 200. It is now cruciform and seats over 450. The altar is against the wall in the front at the far side of the choir. The celebrant's back is to the people when the Eucharist is celebrated and the priest is a long way from the congregation. The arrangement is traditional, with a pulpit and lectern nearer the people.

The parish now has several buildings, the newest an office building just completed. There are also a parish hall, a library, an education wing, and a choir space. These have been added in the past 23 years because the parish has grown from less than 100 members to 680. During this time the parish budget has grown from $18,000 in 1965 to $289,000 in 1987. The increases are remarkable in light of the fact that Peachtree has only doubled in size in that time.

Yet these numbers tell only part of the story. The parish has had a collateral growth in activity. There is a large church school, three worship services which are well attended, and there are fellowship activities for the young, the old and those in between. In addition, the parish provides key leadership for many community organizations.

The parish would describe itself as traditional. It sees itself as pro-family and conservative in theology, yet it uses the 1979 prayer book. Spiritual growth is at the core of the congregation's life and members can speak at great length about how they have grown in the faith through their association with Christ Church.

The mission and ministry of the people are growing as well. Everyone seems to be doing something, whether visiting the sick, teaching church school or greeting newcomers. All this grows out of an understanding of lay ministry and spiritual responsibility. Dr. Frost often asks people to do things and he is also fond of saying, "This is your parish, not mine." This statement is owned by many, if not all of the members.

The parish has three worship services. The 8 a.m. service is attended by an average of 50 people and is a simple service. At 9:30 a.m. there is a family service with an attendance of about 100 on a typical Sunday. This service precedes the church school time and most of the children in the parish attend it. Its focus is on the children and a simple homily is delivered for them by the rector or the associate. Finally, the 11 a.m. service draws over 200 to a traditional service with music and choir, a service which alternates Morning Prayer and Eucharist, depending on the Sunday.

Christ Church has a large staff, mostly lay people. They are a full time parish coordinator, a secretary, a director of religious education (DRE), a typist, an organist and choir director who is part time, and a part-time bookkeeper. Besides being paid staff members, this team, as Dr. Frost calls them, are members of the parish who are highly committed to the ministry of the whole community. Usually there is also an

12

ordained assistant to the rector, but at the time I visited this position was vacant. It is Dr. Frost's idea that the role of these people is to coordinate with him the lay ministry of Christ Church, and they do. The parish is a powerhouse, teaching the faith, growing and empowering its members to care for one another and to go out into the world in Christ's name.

The Church of Our Savior on John's Island was founded eight years ago as a mission of the Diocese of South Carolina. It has had one priest in charge, the Rev. Ladson F. Mills III. Serving primarily the retirement communities of Seabrook and Kiawah, Our Savior has grown from 35 families using the chapel at Camp St. Christopher on Seabrook to a parish with 284 members in less than eight years. A new church seating 350 has just been completed, located between a convenience store and a mobile home, outside the security gates of Kiawah and Seabrook. This was done to remind the parish that they serve the people who live outside the gates as well as those within. In the first year the mission had a budget of $42,000 of which $38,000 was pledged. It now has a budget of $152,000 of which $135,000 is pledged.

Our Savior has a single worship service, a Eucharist, at 9 a.m., attended by an average of 170. A very small church school and adult education forum follows the service. As the communities the parish serves are mostly retirees there is not a lot of concern about the lack of a church school in the traditional sense. The children who are members of the parish serve as acolytes and this role seems to suit them well.

The focus of the life of the parish is service to one another and to the people of John's Island, most of whom are black and live either in poverty or close to it. The church has an extensive tutoring program at the local high school, a clothing drop off, and is involved in Habitat for Humanity on John's Island, and in most of the social service projects on the island. Members visit the sick and rally around one another in times of crisis. It is symbolic of this parish's commitment to service that the church was built as a large square building with removable chairs so that it can serve as a hurricane shelter.

Holy Cross/Faith Memorial Church in Pawley's Island, South Carolina, is the smallest of the six parishes. A black parish with 33 adult communicants in good standing, its history goes back to the slave chapels of the ante-bellum South. It has always been a parish dedicated to outreach and has been associated with a diocesan camp and with the Faith Memorial School, both of which have shared a piece of property with the church for the last 45 years. The parish had been served only part time by clergy for many years and so the core of the leadership had come from the lay readers until three years ago. At that time the parish called the Rev. Antoine Campbell to serve as vicar and director of Episcopal Outreach of Pawley's Island, the umbrella organization which oversees the parish's outreach. Holy Cross/Faith Memorial Church has been called by its vicar "a family-sized parish with a corporation-sized ministry." In the last three years Episcopal Outreach of Pawley's Island has added a nutrition program for the elderly, a free medical clinic, a black heritage festival, and is beginning to work on building moderate and low income housing for the poor. This is important because Pawley's Island is rapidly developing into another affluent retirement community and the poorer original residents are being forced out by increased housing costs.

Yet the parish is more than a social outreach organization. The members take seriously their stewardship of the life of the parish. In the past three years the pledged income has gone up 25 per cent, from $7,500 to $10,000 per year. This is significant, given the fact that the parish has not seen any marked growth in adult membership during that time. The parish is reaching out, beginning a church school for children on the island. These children are picked up in a

15-passenger van. After church school, they attend worship with the adults.

Holy Cross/Faith Memorial Church engages in a powerful ministry, even more remarkable given the constant decline in the black population of Pawley's Island and the fact that with only 33 adult members and a budget of $26,500 they provide the core leadership for an outreach ministry with an annual budget over ten times that size.

St. George's Church in York Harbor, Maine, is situated in one of the oldest resort communities in the country. York Harbor was once the rival of Newport, Rhode Island, for the title of most exclusive resort in New England. This was in the 1920s, before the Depression. The parish has had the same rector, the Rev. David Holroyd, for 16 years and during that time has grown considerably faster that the town. In 1977 the parish had 118 families giving $29,000 to a parish budget of $36,000. In 1987 the budget was $147,000, with $104,000 of that being given by 170 families. The number of members has gone from 235 to 508 in ten years and the worship attendance has gone from an average of 58 people on a Sunday to over 150.

Members feel they have been blessed financially and give about 25 per cent of their budget to outreach projects with the goal of eventually giving 50 per cent very much a parish priority. In 1982 the church building was moved from a narrow piece of land in a commercial section of York Harbor to a new location on the corner of Clark's Lane. This move enabled the parish to add a much needed undercroft and parish hall to the existing structure. Everyone at St. George's regards the parish house as a community resource and so the building is left open almost all the time for prayer and meditation.

The Church of the Good Shepherd in Rangeley, Maine, is exceptional because it is a middle-sized/pastoral church in an isolated town of 1,200 in western Maine. Forty minutes from the nearest McDonald's and the nearest hospital, one would expect the community to be served by a struggling mission with a part-time priest. This is the case in both the Roman Catholic and Congregational churches. Yet the Church of the Good Shepherd has a full-time priest, the Rev. K. Holly Eden, and is a full-fledged parish with an extensive ministry to the town and to its own members. The building itself is large, beautiful and well maintained. This is seen by the members of the parish as a symbol of their commitment to the community. Many groups use the parish hall, the largest in the town available for use by voluntary groups. The building is in use every night and day. The parish budget doubled in ten years while the membership remained about the same size. This parish has grown less than the Church of our Savior, Christ Church or St. George's but its mission and ministry are excellent given the fact that Rangeley has not grown at all. If anything, the community has been losing ground as the children who grew up there find themselves having to leave in order to find work. This is another church which is never locked, a sign that people are welcome any time.

St. Bartholomew's in Yarmouth, Maine, has perhaps the most spectacular record of growth. The parish was founded as a mission in 1973 but had some ups and downs. It was down to ten active families in 1982 and decided as a venture in faith to call a full time vicar. At that time the church was meeting in a converted gas station. Six years later the congregation had a new building. St. Bartholomew's grew to 238 members and was admitted as a parish by the Diocese of Maine in May of 1988. The church describes itself as a place where people can care for one another, be accepted as they are, and learn to grow in faith. The church building is overfilled each Sunday with more that 100 people at worship and the feeling of community is strong. The parish reaches out to the poor and to one another, but its strength is in reaching out to newcomers. It has done this so well that there is some jealousy reported by the local clergy.

St. Bartholomew's is a place where lay ministry is valued. The rector, the Rev. Gil Birney, spends most of his time visiting new people and the sick and needy, so much of the work of the parish is done by lay people through committees. Gil states that the growth of the parish is due to the laity and this seems to be the case, but his contribution is important too.

These six parishes have done much better than one would expect, given their surroundings. Three are in rapidly growing communities, and have grown much more than the surrounding areas. Two are in declining areas and have held their own in terms of numbers, and increased their activities in terms of mission work. One is in an area experiencing slow growth, and has grown "slowly but steadily" over the years. All have outstanding records of ministry to persons both within and without their parish families. In every parish people speak of growing in their faith and ministry as servants of Jesus Christ and manifest that growth through their works in the parish and the community.

THE RESEARCH DESIGN

It is easy to be descriptive and much more could be said about these parishes if this were a case study book, but the deeper question is why are these parishes thriving when others in similar circumstances are not? It was in order to answer this question that a research design was developed which would enable a deeper understanding of the dynamics of each parish. This design used five types of data: statistical information from the parochial reports of ten years, five years, and one year back; a questionnaire which was sent to the clergy staff and twenty key lay leaders identified by the rector or vicar; ninety-minute interviews with the clergy, key lay leaders, a long time member and a new member; observation of the parish on a Sunday morning; and open forums after each worship service with anyone who wished to attend.

The parochial report is a document prepared each year by every parish and mission of the Episcopal Church. It is a national document with the same format for every church. It contains information about number of members, budget, amount of money pledged and by how many people, the number and types of services and the changes in the number of members. By looking at these statistics it is easy to document the changes taking place in any parish or mission over time.

The questionnaire used was the Parish Planning Inventory developed by the Center for Social and Religious Research of the Hartford Seminary Foundation. This survey contains 181 questions on all aspects of parish life. Areas covered include the tasks of the church, organizational characteristics, congregational identity, the tasks of the pastor, facilities, Christian education for adults and children, worship, sermons, community involvement, stewardship, and evangelism. A final section asks about the respondent. Questions include age, income, religious beliefs, level of church participation, and background information about income, employment, gender and household. Many of the questions have rating scales from low to high enabling a qualitative analysis. These questionnaires were computer scored both for each church and for the sample as a whole.

The clergy were interviewed individually. They were asked about their personal background, how they came to the parish, how they viewed the parish, their role in the parish, the characterization of the parish as excellent by their bishop, and the genius of the parish, the single key characteristic which made this particular parish outstanding. Special attention was paid to being comprehensive in these interviews so that no area of parish life was neglected. In this way stewardship, conflict, worship, theology, mission, kind of people, the typical work week, training, sermon preparation, morale, and the role of lay leadership were all discussed.

The lay leaders were interviewed in groups of ten. Many questions were the same as those asked the clergy. In addition they were asked why they were members of this particular parish and to give a brief history of the parish.

The newcomers and oldtimers were asked to describe the parish and their view of it. In the open forums only one question was asked: "This parish has been characterized by the bishop as excellent. Do you agree and if you do why do you think this is so?"

Large volumes of information were gathered. Over 120 persons were interviewed in depth and several hundred participated in the open forums. The process showed both the uniqueness of each parish and startling similarities.

Again, the three constants were: First, the faith is effectively taught and lived. Second, there is a single focus for the common life of the community which provides a channel for the energy and vision of the community. Third, each parish has outstanding lay and ordained leadership and it is the latter which is key. Outstanding clerical leadership precedes and empowers the outstanding lay leadership. It enables "ordinary" lay people to become extraordinary Christian leaders.

I believe that any parish in which these three are present will become excellent over time.

Teaching the faith

It is popular in non-churchgoing circles to say that people go to church to be seen, to sell real estate, to assuage the guilt they have for being such bad people during the week. And it is popular in church circles for people to say that they are a part of a church because of all that it does, the mission outreach, the fellowship, the service to the poor, the nurture of children.

The latter description of the work of the church is to a certain extent true of the six parishes in this study. It was so common in one parish that I asked: "So tell me, what is the difference between this parish and the Red Cross. You both do good works, you both find that the members are people who are fun to work with, and you are both concerned about the life of the community beyond the walls of the parish. What *is* the difference?"

This question produced an explosion of indignation, for in the minds of the people of these parishes there is a profound difference. "We come here to worship Jesus Christ and to learn to live better lives," one woman replied angrily. "We come here to increase our faith," responded a sixty-year-old altar guild director. "This is where we find God," was the simple and heart-felt statement of one senior warden. "In this parish God comes first," said another person. In each study parish the deepening of one's personal relationship with God was the central reason for participating in the life of that Christian community.

"How is this done?" was the next question. The response was that the deepening of one's faith came through the relationship one had with the priest and from one's relationship with other people in the parish. The latter will be the subject of the next chapter.

The priest's role in the deepening of the spiritual lives of those interviewed had three parts:

First, people found that listening to the Sunday morning sermon was the key to deepening their faith; everything else came from it. In all six parishes the sermon style was seen as being as important as the content. The sermons were short, had a single main point, came out of the Bible lessons for the week and were relevant to the daily lives of the congregation.

Second, some members of the parish were involved with some sort of small group study which was intense. This was a weekly meeting which varied as to its content but had as its focus the deepening of one's personal faith life. It was not oriented toward some specific program objective. This was usually led by the rector or vicar, but not always.

Third, the people cited personal contact with the parish priest as a key area of growth for them. This contact was centered in conversation, which might take place almost anywhere, but usually in the context of visitation in the home or the hospital.

TEACHING THROUGH SERMONS

The Sunday sermon is the core of the teaching ministry in these successful parishes.

In my interview sessions with lay leaders I began by asking them to describe how long they had been a member of the parish and why they attended that particular parish instead of another or none at all. Two kinds of remarks were common. First, the community was seen as friendly. Second, the clerical staff, especially the priest in charge, was seen as setting a climate in which it was easy to be a Christian. When asked how this was done, again and again those questioned mentioned the sermon.

"He gives us the meaning of the church in a loving and caring way," said one person about Ladson Mills' sermons. Another saw John Frost's as being "relevant in a day to day way." "Each week I am helped to take a step in the right direction," was a comment on Gil Birney's homilies. "He directs me to a spiritual faith I didn't know I had before," was another. David Holroyd's sermons were described as "low key but to the point." "He helps by not letting you off the hook," said one. Another commented that mention of sin had made a reappearance and that she appreciated it. "This is how we are and this is how we can do better," was how she phrased it. He also "preaches as if he expects you to listen and so you do."

And so the sermons were important and valued. That in and of itself is not surprising. What is surprising is the commonality of sermon style found in the six parishes and the common expectations revealed in the questionnaire responses from the lay leaders. Each lay leader was asked to complete the 181-question Parish Planning Inventory published by the Hartford Seminary Foundation. One of the sections of the questionnaire concerned the sermon.

The most important quality of all, the number one priority, was that the sermon "touches on my everyday life." The people spoke over and over about how homey stories about family and encounters in the supermarket and thoughts on such diverse topics as building a house or playing hide and seek in the undercroft or watching a fire burn in the fireplace were at the center of a faith which has applicability in the real world, in the world in which they live.

The second most important quality was that the sermon "be biblically based and illustrated." The people of all the parishes are clear that religious authority comes, for them, from the Bible. They are concerned that the Bible lessons be explained and applied for them in the sermon. They feel that one of the roles of the priest is to make these connections and that the sermon is the best place for this to happen.

Finally, style was important. In most of the parishes people wanted an informal style which made them feel comfortable. None of the clergy studied is a "manuscript" preacher. Each of them works from notes and speaks for a relatively short time. The length of sermon was described as "short but to the point" by one lay leader who could have been speaking for all. The necessity for this style was demonstrated by a lay person who noted that his only criticism of the rector's sermons was that sometimes he "made his point and then forgot to stop."

Some of the negatives from the surveys and interviews are worth noting. The least important quality of a sermon was that it be scholarly! In fact people were worried about getting confused if the sermon were too complex. In a sense this reflects the fact that most people are still the equivalent of sixth-grade Christians: they have not put nearly the time and effort into their lives as Christians as they have put into their roles as parents or business people.

They were not concerned that the preacher set out the various sides of an issue from the pulpit. When I asked about this the response was often, well, that can be covered another Sunday. It was felt that over time all the bases could be covered. In some congregations, especially Christ Church, which labels itself as "a conservative, traditional parish," the need for clear religious authority was given high marks, but it was not given nearly the priority which relevance to day to day life was.

This data was reinforced by my experience of worship with the six congregations. *If you had transcribed the six sermons and handed them out to people you would have been unable to identify which priest had given which sermon and where they were preached!* I heard stories about fires and houses and hide and seek and love for one another and how hard that is and about how much there is to read in a given week and about sheep. In each parish the sermon ran from 10 to 15 minutes, with one exception in which the sermon was closer to 20. In each parish there was some humorous story, usually with the preacher as the target. And in each place the emphasis was on the acutely human aspects of living out the demands of the gospel day to day.

That this was not a random pattern was revealed in the clergy interviews. Each priest sought to make the gospel real through sermons. The technique was to read the scriptures early in the week and then to meditate on them as one went about the tasks of the week. At the end of the week several hours were spent pulling the homily together. The goal was to find ways in which the incidents of the week related to the message of the gospel. It was preaching which came out of life and not out of books.

The sermons also tended to emphasize the positive aspects of the faith. "We don't hear a lot of judgment and that is good," said a member of the Church of Our Savior. "I know that I am a sinner but that I can do better; that is what I get out of sermons," a person at St. Bartholomew's commented. This emphasis on the positive, on the ability of people to do good and do better seems to liberate people for acts of service, to reach out into the wider community. The clergy are aware of this and seek to keep to the formula which works.

This formula is also intensely biblical. Jesus often taught through stories of real life which pointed to God's actions in the world. This is the nature of the parable and its interpretation. In fact this is such a large part of Jesus' teaching style that St. Matthew says that "He said nothing to them without a parable." (13:34) These clergy are following tradition, and it works. People come to church eager to hear what the clergy have to say. "I can't read the bulletin during the sermon any more!" was a humorous but positive comment from a member of St. George's. Few people do in these parishes.

Few clergy or laity felt any need for sermons which were scholarly or overtly political. "People are allowed to make their own decisions here," was a comment I heard often. The clergy said that they do sometimes speak on a topic such as AIDS but that they feel the need to focus on the personal aspects of faith. This focus does have corporate results. The people of the congregations find that by seeking to deepen their personal faith they are strengthened for acts of service. "How could you not reach out?" one person commented. They find they are enabled through being affirmed.

The sermon is at the core of the success of these parishes. The worship I attended was quite diverse. I went to almost a dozen services over the six weeks and they ranged from sung Eucharists to said Morning Prayer. Some had acolytes and some did not. Sometimes the priest celebrated facing the people and in some places the priest had his back to the congregation. Yet at every worship service a sermon or homily was given and in every place the worship was described as excellent or very good on the survey questionnaires. When asked why, the people responded, "because of the sermon."

SMALL GROUP STUDY

The sermon was cited as far and away the most important aspect of teaching the faith. In addition, in each parish there was some small-group adult study which was important to a key group. The purpose of this study was a further deepening of their understanding of what it meant to live as Christians. This group might include a high percentage of the congregation, as at Holy Cross/Faith Memorial and St. Bartholomew's, or a fairly small portion, as for example at Christ Church, but it was seen as an opportunity for those who wished to go deeper than they could as individuals.

Two parishes, St. Bartholomew's and the Church of the Good Shepherd, used the Kerygma Bible Study series published by Trinity Episcopal School for Ministry in Ambridge, Pennsylvania. At Good Shepherd the study group of about ten met on a weekday morning. "It really makes you look at the Bible and learn about it," was one

33

comment. In this parish there was no expectation that everyone take this year-long course, but many people spoke highly of it, even those who were not participants.

At St. Bartholomew's there *was* an expectation that over time everyone in the parish would participate in the course. "There isn't any really strong pressure," one person noted, "but you are sort of expected to take it sooner or later." This same person, who spoke of himself as a gardener by trade, said that while he hadn't wanted to take it, it had helped him a lot. "You get to talk to other people in a way you wouldn't otherwise," and this was helpful. In both parishes the study was led by the rector.

At Christ Church the small group study was a lay-led Bible study on Sunday mornings. This group was aided by the rector or the assistant as needed but was primarily the work of the laity. They had no set curriculum and the leadership rotated as people's outside commitments changed. A member of the group would volunteer to lead and he or she would select the method of Bible study the group would use. At the time I visited the group was beginning again with a new leader who had never taught before. "He is doing very well, better than I expected," a member commented. He was helped in this because the group was an important place for sharing and learning to lead, and so they supported one another.

At Holy Cross/Faith Memorial nearly half the adult membership is either teaching church school or attending an adult Bible study which occurs in the church at the same time as the children's church school. Led by two of the lay readers, both of whom give the sermon on occasion, this study is intense and focused on Bible content. Other lay leaders teach a Bible-content-based Sunday school curriculum to the children. All find that this keeps them working on growing in the faith beyond what they might gain from the Sunday sermon.

A prayer and meditation group is the focus of lay study at St. George's Church in York Harbor. This group meets every Monday evening and includes the rector. It is led by a lay person trained as a spiritual director and has been meeting for a couple of years. The people of the parish note that this group has affected the life of the parish through its holding up of the life of prayer and that people can join or drop out as they choose.

At the Church of Our Savior, there is a weekly Bible study on the Sunday lessons, led by the rector. It is very informal and is primarily a guided discussion of the lections for the week.

Each group is held up as being important for the life of the parish. Except for the Kerygma group at St. Bartholomew's there is no pressure to join, but many people do. The study groups are often made up of the lay leaders of the congregation and provide a vital core of deeply committed people. But it is clear from these parishes that focusing on small groups is not the sole key to a vital parish life as some, especially Lyman Coleman of Serendipity, have argued. Groups are seen as important but not foundational for the life of the community.

PERSONAL CONTACT WITH
THE CLERGY

In every parish the personal example of the clergy in daily life was seen as a key aspect of learning about the life of faith. Clergy were seen as having exemplary Christian lives, whose general principles people in the parish sought to emulate. The people had a lot of contact with their clergy, either through pastoral calling, serving on committees together, or through meeting on the street, at the grocery store, or on the golf course. Members found that through their interactions with the clergy their lives as Christians were strengthened.

The first and most powerful aspect of this was the fact that the clergy were not "above the people" in their actions. Most clergy dress informally most of the time and this was seen as a plus by most people. Clergy did wear clerical dress on Sundays and to hospitals but most of the time casual shirts or blouses were the norm. This communicated the powerful message that one did not need to be overly formal or pious to be a good Christian.

The second aspect of learning from the lives of the clergy was their willingness to share their personal struggles with the faith. This inspired others to share their problems both with the clergy and with one another. "Her weakness helps me in my weakness," was how one woman described this aspect of Holly Eden's ministry. People in the parishes needed to hear that the clergy had problems with their children and with their parents. They needed to hear that the clergy did not have the answer to every question and that they, too, often struggled in prayer seeking out the right pathway for their lives and for the life of the parish. They needed to hear that life in the pastor's home was not always a model of bliss but was a lot like their own. They needed to hear that the cars of the clergy break down and that their golf games go off.

These aspects of "humanizing the clergy" were important because the clergy in all these congregations carry a lot of symbolic weight. Many people still have childlike assumptions about the clergy. The clergy can easily become God substitutes in the projective life of the congregation, and so their humanness helps the people under their care to bring the gospel closer to every day life.

The clergy in these congregations do not "let it all hang out" all the time, but they make an effort to be as fully integrated as possible in their lives. This includes their spouses and children. All the clergy spouses in the parishes in this study are active in their congregations, but they are not the overburdened clergy spouses of stereotype. Rather, they are active lay people in their own right who do what they believe their gifts and inclinations call them to. Some sing in the choir, some play instruments, two are very active in the community and do relatively little in the parish. One is a true partner in the ministry and has become the parish secretary at Holy Cross/Faith Memorial, a mission which was too small to have a paid secretary.

All the clergy with children try not to have undue expectations of their children. I was told and observed that their kids cry with the rest, make noise, go to church school, and generally are allowed to be normal. The result is a kind of relief for all concerned. Clergy children are not overburdened with unrealistic expectations for behavior and the parishioners do not have any unrealistic models to try to live up to.

Yet, the clergy do try to live the best Christian lives they can, and their parishioners expect them to. In this I detect no falsity. They are all truly integrated in the psychological sense. They are not superficially pious, but genuinely faithful. They would not describe themselves as saints, yet many of their parishioners would and seek to emulate them in the faithfulness, if not the details, of their lives.

CONCLUSION

The effective teaching of the faith is at the core of the success of these six congregations. The Sunday sermon has a very particular style. It contains a single point, is tightly connected to both the scripture and to the spiritual struggles of everyday life, is informally presented, in most cases is short, and often contains a humorous story. It is the sermon which keeps people coming back, "if only to hear what new crazy idea he is going to come up with this week." People are inspired in a quiet way by this preaching to go out and try to live better lives as Christians. Supporting the preaching are small group study and the everyday observance of the Christian life of the rector and his family by the congregation. It may seem like a burden and a tall order but as one priest noted, "It is not that hard, I just try to be me and let God do the rest."

The community of faith

At a deep level people come to church because they wish to be better Christians, better followers of Jesus Christ. Yet for many it is the quality of the community of faith which draws them in and holds them over time. "There is a sense of community here," was a common comment from lay people in the six study parishes. "This is the most caring community and church I have been in in my life," said one member of the Church of Our Savior. "I came because it felt like one big, lively, involved family," said a member of St. George's. "The people were friendly, open, loving and welcoming," said another member of that parish. A woman who had just joined the Church of the Good Shepherd said that the parish had the "kindest people I have ever met." One person at Christ Church described the parish of 680 members as "friendly and small." A good feeling about the community which begins with the first visit and continues over time is one of the attributes of these strong parishes.

In this chapter I will describe the four attributes of the community of faith in each of these six parishes. First and most important, people are accepted without judgment, as they are. Second, the parish is often described as a family, but "even better," a family with a lot of mutual support and affirmation. Third, the parish handles conflict so well that people use the term disagreement rather than conflict to describe their problems. And fourth, there is a general tone of interaction, set by the priest and the senior lay leaders, which is positive and encouraging.

BEING ACCEPTED WHERE YOU ARE

The single most important quality of the community of faith in these six churches is an acceptance of individuals as unique persons who do not need to change to be welcomed. Regardless of parish size this quality was cited by all as a key prerequisite for feeling comfortable with the parish.

People who join the Episcopal Church come from many backgrounds. Research indicates that over half the current Episcopal Church membership grew up in other Christian traditions. All but one of the parishes fit this pattern. At the Church of Our Savior less than half came from Episcopal Church backgrounds. Other faith traditions were Methodist 27 per cent, Baptist 9 per cent, and Presbyterian 18 per cent. At Christ Church the lifelong Episcopalians were not even a plurality! They constituted only 25 per cent of the sample. The Methodist Church had contributed the most members with 35 per cent. Other denominations represented included Presbyterian 20 per cent, Baptist 15 per cent, and Lutheran 5 per cent. The data is similar for the other parishes except Holy Cross/Faith Memorial where all of the respondents had grown up in the Episcopal tradition. This is largely due to the small size of this church.

This diversity of origins makes it imperative for growing congregations to allow people to come in with few if any requirements beyond attendance at worship. The comments of the members bear this out. One woman at the Church of Our Savior commented, "I know I am a sinner and this parish is a place where I can be helped but not judged." "Everyone is welcome here, and the fact that I, a Baptist, was welcomed here is an example of that," was the remark another made, responded to with chuckles by the others since the speaker was a vestry member. At St. George's Church the mother of a physically and emotionally handicapped child noted that her daughter was loved and encouraged by the congregation. A person at the Church of Our Savior commented that he was "given a sense of confidence and allowed to be who I am." A newcomer to the Church of the Good Shepherd said that she was accepted as a member by the "natives" in the congregation even though they have a reputation for being very suspicious of outsiders from "away."

People are also allowed to be active or inactive as they choose. There is a "unique set of opportunities to fill your own pail or give as you need to here," was a comment about St. George's. "No one forces you to do anything, but you want to," was a remark about Christ Church which could have been echoed by people in most of the parishes. "This is a gas station where you can get tanked up for the week if you need to, or be part of the crew if you want to," was a remark abut St. Bartholomew's, a church then located in a converted gas station.

This does not mean that the content of the gospel is diluted. A member of the Church of the Good Shepherd described it this way: "Our rector presents the gospel the way it should be presented, but then we live and let live." This is a stance which is held in common by all the parishes. People are encouraged to move deeper, but growth in the faith is not made a requirement for membership.

The one parish which is all Episcopalian by origin has found a unique way to reach out and be accepting at the same time. The people of Holy Cross/Faith Memorial realized that as they were getting older and their children were moving away there were fewer and fewer children in the congregation. They wanted to begin a church school. They had tried to recruit new people from Pawley's Island but were not successful. So they asked people if it would be okay to pick up their children and bring them to church and then return them after church school and worship. The parents of the children were enthusiastic and they now have a church school of over a dozen children in a parish which formerly had only two, the vicar's. What is striking about this is the lack of judgment passed on the parents. The parish was reaching out to those who would come, without judging those who would not.

These non-judgmental, inclusive traditions, free people to move forward on their spiritual journey at their own pace. This has allowed for high levels of growth in some of the parishes, and an ability to function with few if any cliques and with a lot of rotation of leadership in all of the parishes as people become interested and available.

LIKE A FAMILY BUT BETTER

In the Parish Planning Inventory which was given to the lay leaders of each study parish, one question asked the respondents to agree or disagree with this statement: "Our congregation feels like one large family." Most of the lay leaders agreed strongly with this statement. The feeling of family was cited often as a reason both for joining a congregation and for staying in it.

This congregational family is affirming and accepting in a way that one's natural family often is not. It comes from hundreds of coffee hour conversations and interactions outside the church. "People from Christ Church don't only say 'hi' to you at church, they come over no matter where you are, in the grocery store, the mall, on the golf course, anywhere." "This is my real family," someone said. At Holy Cross/Faith Memorial Church the mission *really* is one large family, with most of the 30 members related. It is a happy gathering of people who often have lunch together in the parish house after services.

One of the places this family-but-better feeling is manifested is in worship. In all the parishes I visited, during the time of formal prayer, names were spoken freely from the congregation. In several parishes the clergy, at the announcements, noted pastoral needs and ways in which the parish might respond. In a couple of parishes I heard notes of thanks read by the clergy for care given to people in the parish or wider community. In most of the parishes, passing the peace was a time of real greeting and interpersonal contact. People said "hi" to one another; sometimes people moved out of their pews to greet others; the clergy wandered around saying hello, and there was a general feeling of warmth spread throughout those gathered for worship. In the places where this did not happen, there was a traffic-jam in the aisle after the service as people greeted each other then. I asked about this at the most formal and traditional of the parishes, Christ Church, and the very proper treasurer replied, "It's need-driven; we need to greet each other; we just don't do it until the formal worship is over. We value reverence."

Greeting is only one aspect of this extended family style. In parish after parish the need to care for one another in the way we used to associate with blood relatives was seen as a key to their strength. "When my husband died the parish was all around me. I don't know what I would have done without them." "We've shared a lot of tragedies over the years," said a member of the Church of the Good Shepherd. "When one person is hurt, we all hurt," was a comment heard at Holy Cross/Faith Memorial. The community of faith which cares is a dominant image of how the church ought to be, and it is lived out in these six parishes.

This is illustrated by a story told at Christ Church by one of the lay leaders who was interviewed. She had become less active in the past year because her son was in a serious automobile accident which had left him in a coma. "He came home in a class-two coma from the hospital after three weeks. They didn't know if he would wake up. I didn't know what a class-two coma *was* before the accident." She found the parish was more than willing to care for her. "I didn't cook a meal for eight weeks. Not a single meal. Food just kept on appearing at our door. I don't know what we would have eaten otherwise. A lot of hot dogs I guess." Even a year later she has very little energy except for her family's situation, for her son was moved to a rehabilitation hospital some distance away. She is still loved and carried by the congregation and is "taking a lot more than I am giving right now." She had expected that as her involvement as a leader decreased the parish would be less supportive. This has not proved to be the case. The continuing care of the parish is a shining example of how a supportive community should function.

HANDLING CONFLICT

One of the problems which bedevils the Christian church is the seeming inability of many local churches to handle conflict well. Many parishes have gone into crisis because of intense unresolved conflict. This often results in the firing of the clergy and almost always includes a loss of membership and a period of instability.

This problem sometimes arises out of a difference in perception about the nature of the church. Many people assume that because Christians are peace-lovers they should never have disagreements. This forces the disagreements which inevitably occur to be pushed under the surface. They then emerge in all sorts of hidden and inappropriate ways. The malicious gossipy remark which causes a committee chair to quit is a classic example. Most clergy who have served conflicted parishes are familiar with the "whispering campaign" which can disempower parish leadership.

All the parishes in this study were asked specifically how they handled conflict. The general response from lay leaders was, "We don't have conflicts." In their view, an excellent parish was relatively conflict free. This led to the follow-up question of whether the parish ever had disagreements. "Oh yes, all the time!" came the response. What emerged was a picture of parishes which can have intense disagreements but resolve them in the normal process of parish life.

Most of the clergy in charge have similar styles for handling parish conflicts. If the dispute is between persons, they seek to get the parties involved to work with one another to live amicably in the parish. No one is ever asked to leave, but people are given clear guidelines for conduct and expected to follow them. These include speaking up but also seeking to "behave as Christian people." This means remaining in relationship with one another without needing to agree on everything.

A rector told this story: A member of the parish had been angry with a family for not being more active in fund-raising. This particular parish does a lot of fund-raising and seems to enjoy it even though the vast majority of parish funds come from pledging. The organizer let it be known that he was very angry with a family "for not pulling their weight" but he did not confront them directly. This led to discomfort on the part of the family. They decided to confront the complainer and to ask him to stop. But first they went to their rector to tell him what they were going to do. The rector offered to go with them but they declined, saying that they would rather do this themselves. The rector knew this was not the first time the person in question had alien-ated a family through being too aggressive, and resolved to confront the individual himself. So both the family and the rector met with the man about his over-aggressiveness. When he was asked about his behavior he said that it was just that he cared so much about the parish. He said he did not mean to alienate anyone. All the parties involved found they agreed on the need to work to strengthen the parish, and they agreed to disagree about the need for aggressive recruiting of fund-raisers in the service of this goal. The man agreed as well to tone down his recruiting methods as he saw that this was being counter-productive.

This kind of conflict resolution through interpersonal interaction needs a fairly high level of maturity in the individuals involved. In all the parishes under study the priest uses this style and teaches it to the parish, either through coaching the individuals involved or through preaching about it when the lessons are appropriate.

In handling disagreements all of the parishes also used a style which emphasized openness and discussion as part of the decision-making process. The surveys returned all indicated high levels of agreement with the statement that "Disagreements/conflicts are dealt with openly rather than hushed up or hidden behind closed doors." This, coupled with high levels of agreement with the statement that "important decisions are rarely made without a discussion by a broad spectrum of leaders and members," defines the basic conflict management style of the congregations.

"We talk things out," said one vestry member. "I slow the process down when it looks like significant opposition is starting," three of the clergy said. "We scream and shout and stand toe to toe and when it is over hug each other," said a senior warden somewhat, but not entirely, metaphorically.

All the parish leaders cited maturity as a key factor in conflict resolution. "We have all been in disagreements before," noted one person. And because they value their relationships with one another, they are committed to resolving conflicts.

The clergy are important in this process. Holly Eden was described as a "conflict manager and facilitator." "She lets us work it out for ourselves," one vestry member commented. All of the clergy cited the need to know when to take stands, when to back down, and when to force others to work with one another to resolve their conflicts. They saw this skill in discernment as the key when coupled with the maturity of the congregation.

One example from the Church of Our Savior will serve to illustrate these points. The congregation was building a new church. They had decided to build a bell tower but there was considerable disagreement about whether the bell tower should be attached to the church or not. The architect told the vestry that either would be fine, that the cost would be the same. It was up to the parish to decide. The discussion grew quite heated. "I really don't care," said the rector, and so he resolved to focus on helping the vestry to reach a decision. People's voices began to be raised and at 11:30 p.m. there was some shouting and some angry remarks. "This meeting is adjourned," said the rector. "I want you to go home and pray about this situation and then come back tomorrow at 1:30 to decide. Spend that time on your knees if you need to, but this yelling has got to stop."

Several of the principals in this drama, who told me the story, said they had never seen their rector so angry and that over the ensuing night and day of prayer they realized that the bell tower location was not worth splitting the church or destroying friendships for. They felt that they were not modeling Christian behavior and they wished to. The rector said he was worried but had acted to restore the foundation for the vestry's work, which was faithful prayer.

The next day the decision was made in fairly short order. Some members of the vestry at that time cannot now remember how they felt. Some do, especially those who felt strongly that the bell tower should be attached to the church rather than be free-standing as it is now. "But it really is a little thing when you put it in perspective," one person commented.

This combination of maturity, modeling, openness and prayer seems to make the life of these parishes nearly free of destructive conflicts.

SETTING THE TONE

One further aspect of the life in these six parishes needs to be discussed. This is the role of the clergyperson in setting the tone for the whole church. Over and over the clergy were cited as the key to the lovingness of the parish. "We reflect our rector's personality; he is loving and so are we," was a remark made about David Holroyd. "Gil is willing to share his struggles with us and so we can better share them with one another," was a comment about Gil Birney. "Holly shows her weakness and lets us minister to her and so I am able to be weak and cared for also," one vestry person at the Church of the Good Shepherd said. "He loves us and so we love one another," was a comment made about John Frost.

The clergypersons *do* set the tone for the whole parish. If they are open and willing to risk so is the parish. If they are angry or depressed the parish will reflect this. This seems a heavy burden to place on the clergy, but it is real and almost all the parishes noted it. If a parish is loving and open it is highly likely that they will have an open and loving pastor. I will say more about the whys of this in the chapter on leadership.

CONCLUSION

Less obvious than preaching or adult classes, the community of faith, the tone of relationships, is nonetheless the first thing people notice when they visit a parish for the first time. The clergy set the tone, model good conflict management styles and lead by example. At the same time the congregation seeks that kind of leadership and responds well, trying to live "better lives as Christians" using the models held up by the clergy and the lay leaders.

The important element is meeting people where they are and accepting them for who they are. "This is the most loving and accepting parish I have ever been in," was a common remark made by newcomers to these parishes. Some had experienced this kind of community in churches of other traditions, and they all felt the formula was the same. If people feel judged as they arrive they will most often not stay. Yet the standards of the faith need to be clearly taught; a delicate balance must be struck. In each of the six parishes in this study it has been.

Focus

In each parish in this study there is a single, specific focus for the life of the congregation, very important to congregational health. In each congregation there has evolved, sometimes intentionally, sometimes organically, an activity in which the congregation finds the best expression of its mission. This focus comes to dominate the conversation, planning and activity of the parish. It becomes the area where many of the most committed people become involved, and it tends to get the most air time during the announcements and space in the newsletter. When one interviews members of the congregation about their common life it is the issue and activity most often discussed.

This focus may not be a formal "mission imperative" written out and posted for all to see. Some of the six churches have accepted the statement of mission found in the Book of Common Prayer as their mission statement: "The mission of the Church is to restore all people to unity with God and each other in Christ." (p. 855) However, the statement from the BCP is too global for lay people who wish to be engaged in specific activities in the service of God and the church.

Most parishes have something which they "do best," but that is different from the focus I am speaking of here. The focus in these congregations is not general, such as "serving the needy." It is specific, as serving the poor of John's Island through tutoring in the local high school, building low cost housing through Habitat for Humanity, providing clothing and furniture at need, and pushing for ecumenical cooperation in all aspects of mission work on the island. Each of the six parishes has such a specific focus for their common life.

These congregations do engage in the traditional broad range of parish activities. Those with lots of children have church school; pastoral care and worship are important in all of them; they work at stewardship and evangelization and are engaged in adult education. However, there is, in addition, in each church a single focal point which serves as inspiration for the whole community, even for those people not engaged in the work directly.

MISSION TO THE COMMUNITY
VIA HANDS-ON ACTIVITY
• THE CHURCH OF OUR SAVIOR

As I arrived on John's Island, South Carolina, to visit the Church of Our Savior, I was impressed by the new church building, only recently occupied. The large white stucco building was airy and well appointed. Located outside the gates of the planned communities of Kiawah and Seabrook, it was easily accessible to all the people of the island, black and white, affluent and poor. The building was the result of a lot of time, planning and money.

I expected to find that building had been the center of parish life for the previous three years. This was not the case.

The first indication came from Betty Stringfellow, one of the oldest members, resident of John's Island since 1984 and during the summers for many years before that. When I asked her what was the primary focus of the parish, she spoke of outreach to the poor of John's Island: "The people who moved to Kiawah and Seabrook saw it as retirement, golf and bridge; it didn't work out that way." When they arrived they were "shocked by the poverty on the island," and decided to reach out. In this she has been active, referring to her home as the "half-way house, half-way between the rich and the poor."

Reaching out has taken many forms. Most are ecumenical. The parish is not interested in using their ministry of service to become the dominant ecclesiastical power on the island. Rather they see their involvement as drawing all people of faith together in meeting the needs of the poor.

Some of the needs are basic services. A used clothing center has been set up and the annual rummage sale is a community event. "They bring people in by the bus load," remarked one member. If a family needs furniture the word goes out and the pieces are left on Betty's porch or at the St. Francis-Hebron Center, a Roman Catholic help mission, and the needy take what they need. One year the island people who had wood stoves but were too weak to chop wood were identified and the people of the parish chopped wood and delivered a winter's supply to several families. The parish initiated a meals-on-wheels program which now has 12 drivers.

The use of the rector's discretionary fund is a big part of this ministry. If a person needs glasses the word goes out and the priest provides the funds. If there is need for transportation due to an emergency, it is taken care of. Members give to the fund and the priest tells them how he uses it.

The parish began a "toys for grandmothers" program so that older people on the island could buy toys at 5 per cent of cost for their grandchildren, enabling them to have a more joyful Christmas than otherwise might be possible. The parish also initiated a free community dinner on the Wednesday evening before Thanksgiving, served by the members of the parish. Why at that time? So that "the people who serve Thanksgiving dinner to others could themselves be served."

The parish sponsors a kindergarten for black children on the island to help them get a good start for elementary school. Perhaps the area which brings greatest pride to parish members to whom I spoke is the tutoring program at the public high school, an institution not known for high quality. Several members realized that young people graduating from the school were ill prepared, their reading and math skills often substandard. They intervened with a one-on-one tutoring program for juniors and seniors. They sought help from the city of Charleston, but none was forthcoming, so they proceeded themselves and one and one-half years later they have 22 tutors. Not all are from the Church of Our Savior. It is a great source of pride to the parish that two students who were in the tutoring program have realized that they could go to college and have now been admitted for the fall.

Finally, the church has sought to increase the pride of the people of the island in their culture by sponsoring a natural history group which promotes performances of plays such as the "Devil's Funeral," which is native to the island and in an oral tradition over 100 years old.

61

This group has also sponsored gospel sings at which it is common to have 200 people. The people of the parish report that they are most excited by the cooperation between the black churches and the white churches on the island which this has fostered. In an area where the races have remained culturally separate for hundreds of years, this is no mean feat.

I posed the question, "So you've just built a new church, that must have been the center of your life for the past few years, huh?" "No!" was the emphatic response. "The church building is just a means to an end," one vestry member commented. He continued, "When we built this church we were aware that we needed a bigger and more beautiful worship space, and we have that, but most of all this church is a symbol of our real purpose, to reach out to the people of the island. It has movable chairs so that it can be a hurricane shelter if needed, and it is located outside the gates so that people can come here anytime they want. That is why we built this church, to serve our mission in the community."

OUTREACH TO NEWCOMERS
• ST. BARTHOLOMEW'S

Seven years ago, the service book at St. Bartholomew's reveals, eleven people attended the Christmas Eve service. The mission, begun eight years earlier, had hit bottom. Acknowledging a crisis, they asked for a new part-time pastor and began the process of discerning God's will for the parish.

This small group began to grow and felt God was calling them to change, to take a chance, to seek new horizons. They decided to call a full-time vicar. The bishop's committee decided to assume that the congregation would grow in numbers, faith and ministry. They knew that if they did not take this risk they would surely not grow and might even close.

On Easter Sunday, 1987, there were 210 people at worship, overfilling the converted gas station in which the congregation was then housed. New people came every week and the congregation built a new church, deliberately modest in size. The people of St. Bart's feel that if they grow too large for this new space they would rather build a second church and foster another mission congregation rather than risk losing the sense of intimacy they now have.

This growth is not just a happy accident. The congregation has not experienced a four-fold increase in the number of families in the past five years because they have focused on stewardship as their primary concern. St. Bart's has grown because the welcoming of new people and their incorporation into the life of the congregation is at the heart of their ministry, the major focus of congregational life.

While St. Bart's describes itself in all of its literature as "A Church on the Move!" the congregation has not accepted growth as its primary mission objective. Rather the goal is being faithful to the mandates of the gospel. If this seems ordinary, parish activity proves otherwise.

One sign is Gil Birney's description of his work. When I asked him to describe his role in the parish, his first words were,"I am the worm at the end of the hook." He sees himself as the "point man" in bringing in newcomers. He devotes a large amount of his time to greeting newcomers and visiting them quickly after they visit the parish for worship. He feels the work which best describes the parish is "growing."

The vicar could spend his time in many ways. He has no secretary and could easily have become bogged down in administrative details, or in the new building and the decisions around that. But this work was given to committees and Gil has continued to focus on what he does best, preaching, reaching out, and teaching the adults. The organizational details are left to the laity.

Father Birney may be the worm, but the people of the parish are certainly active participants in the congregation's growth. Of the group which responded to the questionnaire, 87 per cent had invited two or more new families to visit or join the church in the past year. Over one-tenth of the group had invited five or more families to come! If just this group is considered by themselves they have invited over 45 families to visit or join the church! In a congregation of only 115 households this is extraordinary.

Once new people come to church the process of inclusion continues. Parishioners described themselves over and over as risk-takers, not only taking financial risks, such as building the new church, but interpersonal risks. When a person comes into St. Bart's they are warmly greeted. People seek out newcomers and try to make them welcome. "People made the effort to learn our names," said one new member.

And it goes beyond that. One very shy member of the parish told me "I feel guilty if I don't go up to at least one new person each Sunday and introduce myself." He continued, "And that is very hard for me. I don't usually like to mix with people, but here you feel you need to." I asked if he had found meeting people unpleasant. "No, I like it, but it is still hard." It is a tribute to the focus of St. Bart's on newcomers that even shy people get involved in greeting newcomers.

The dress of members is informal and "not stuffy." The style of the church is described as "clear, simplistic and flexible." Another word used is "unselfconscious." This allows people of diverse backgrounds and attitudes to come to St. Bart's and feel included. "We allow people to be individuals and experience God in their own way."

Someone summarized it this way: "You don't have to be perfect, you can be yourself and hold the faith. In other churches I have been a member of, there was a conflict between being a 'Christian' and being yourself. Here that is not so. You don't have to hide your failures here and so you can be welcomed for who you are."

Once people are greeted, they become involved in the parish quickly. "Everyone is important and asked to be involved." Because of the smallness of the space in the old building, people were encouraged to help the very first day. At the end of the main worship service the chairs in the worship space were stacked to make room for coffee hour. The church had only one room and a vestibule and so the worship area doubled as the parish hall/meeting room/office and everything else. Several people reported that the process of stacking up the chairs after worship made them feel a part of the parish immediately. "We feel needed and that is good," remarked one new person. People stayed for coffee and got to know one another.

St. Bart's is involved in a number of different areas of mission and ministry. They have an organized nursing home ministry, they give food to the food bank, the parish gives space to a small day care center during the week. They have the usual number of committees and do the necessary tasks of routine parish ministry very well. Yet it is their focus on gaining new people and helping them become part of the parish which makes St. Bart's unique and is a large part of the excellence of this community of Christians. They are proud of their expansion and they have a burning desire to spread the good news which they have found to others.

PROVIDING THE SOUL FOR A LARGE OUTREACH MINISTRY
• HOLY CROSS/FAITH MEMORIAL

Holy Cross/Faith Memorial has only 33 adult members and a budget of $26,500, of which almost $10,000 comes from the Diocese of South Carolina. On the same property as the church, using many of the same buildings, is Episcopal Outreach of Pawley's Island (EOPI), a ministry to the poor people of the island which includes a medical clinic, a school, a nutrition program for the elderly, a clothes closet, a transportation service, a cultural heritage festival, a summer work camp to provide labor to repair the homes of the poor elderly, and a summer camp for the educationally and emotionally handicapped. EOPI has a budget of over $330,000. The people of Holy Cross/Faith Memorial provide much of the oversight of EOPI. It is here that this unique mission finds its focus.

One day I asked the vicar, the Rev. Antoine Campbell, "How can you balance the needs of the mission, which is a half-time job, with the needs of Episcopal Outreach of Pawley's Island which is a one-and-one half time job?" "It is very busy," Tony replied, "but not all that difficult. The two have so much overlap that doing one seems like doing the other. For example: On Sunday I saw the whole parish at worship and we had lunch together. Then on Monday there was a meeting to plan the Black Heritage Festival and I saw five members of the congregation at that meeting. The next night we had an Episcopal Outreach of Pawley's Island board meeting and I saw another ten members of the congregation. In doing one I often find I am doing the other."

The people of the mission share the pride of their vicar at this partnership. They see it as a seamless whole. It begins on Sunday. "Coming to church and listening to the gospel is the feast, the rest of the week feeds on Sunday." The rest of the week often includes EOPI work and outreach. The people of Holy Cross/Faith Memorial attend board meetings, organize the black community, support the fund-raising efforts of the various ministries and back the vicar as he works to enable and fund EOPI.

This is seen as a natural outgrowth of the day to day following of the gospel heard on Sunday. "The church leads the camp, not the camp the church." This refers to Camp Baskerville, the property the mission and EOPI share. Following the gospel has led the people to Holy Cross/Faith Memorial to reach out in new ways, through a housing corporation which is just beginning, and through a black business people's organization founded by lay readers, now one of the most powerful voices of the black community on the island.

It might seem that with so few people the danger of burn-out would be acute. This is not so. "Many of us went to the school (Faith Memorial School, located on the grounds of EOPI) and our families went there and so this is our life." The people of the church have always been a part of the ministry of EOPI and so it seems natural. Conversation about the upcoming heritage festival dominated coffee hour the week I visited. Some issue relating to ministry almost always does.

One might suppose that with the arrival of a

part-time vicar to run both EOPI and the church that conflict between the two would be an issue. To some extent this is true, but feedback from the members of the parish is that both are stronger because of being better staffed. Holy Cross/ Faith Memorial was unique among the six churches in this study in saying that one of the principal roles of the clergy was to represent the church to the wider community. The church community has an investment in EOPI, and sees Tony's travels in support of this ministry as natural and appropriate.

Since his arrival four years ago both EOPI and Holy Cross/Faith Memorial have grown. EOPI has moved from being the camp in the summer and the school in the winter to being a year-round operation which is a model for others. The parish has increased its financial support of its own ministry 25 per cent and the average number of people at worship has shown a similar increase to 33. Church members are enthusiastic about their ministry and see themselves as making a real difference in the lives of many. EOPI is the focus of the ministry of Holy Cross/Faith Memorial Church and as such is a source of their excellence.

ACTIVITY AND THE BUILDING OF
COMMUNITY IN A LARGE PARISH
• CHRIST CHURCH

"Everyone gets involved very quickly here."
That is important to the success of Christ Church
in Peachtree. This parish of almost 700 members
makes a point of getting people involved quickly
and then helping them to succeed in their en-
deavors.

"I sign them up quickly," the rector, the Rev.
Dr. John Frost, said. "If people come, they want
to get involved." The range of formal involve-
ments focuses mostly on the congregation, but
reaches out informally into the community as
well.

One of the highlights is the "Priesthood of all
Believers," a weekly elderly care program which
involves a lot of the younger members as well.
They meet once a week for lunch and commun-
ion. In addition, they reach out to the sick and
shut-in via cards and visits. Special attention is
given those who have recently lost a loved one.
The church school, an undertaking involving 22
teachers who work in teams to lead over 200
students, is another focus. There is also a
vacation Bible school each summer.

The Parish Visitation Committee reaches
out to new people, visitors, those in the hospital
and those in nursing homes. This is a vital and

vibrant ministry for those "blessed with the gift of hospitality."

When I visited, "E'GODS" was mentioned by almost everyone. The Episcopal Group of Dining and Socializing meets twice a year as a way of building community in this large parish. Initiated by some of the younger members, this group has taken off. The planning of each event, for example a progressive dinner, takes up several months for the steering committee, and the process itself is seen as lots of fun.

The parish also has a large group of church-women and active youth groups.

Many large parishes have such a collection of organizations and committees, but at Christ Church this is the focus which contributes to its excellence. Members talk with enthusiasm about working for the parish as one of the reasons they enjoy being in it. In interview after interview people cited involvement as the key to being a part of Christ Church. "People are enthusiastic and helpful here." "If you say that you are interested in doing something, you can count on getting a call from the office asking you to do just that." "This is a lively place where everyone is involved." "We have a good sense of camaraderie and that is what I love about his place." "Once you have worked with someone, they say 'hi' to you no matter where you are; this is not just a

Sunday church."

This involvement is to a large extent a result of the theology of the rector. "Dr. Frost works very hard, but he lets you know that this is your church not his," said a lay leader. The rector feels that the people are "responsible for the reputation and expansion of Christ Church" and seeks to keep this concept before them. And they do own it.

An example is the staffing pattern at Christ Church. The church has five full-time and three part-time employees. Only two are ordained; the rest are lay members of the congregation. Their function is seen as coordinating the ministry of Christ Church. The lay staff consists of two secretaries and the lay parish coordinator, a woman who has been in the parish over 20 years as both secretary and member. "Sooner or later everything comes through the office," was her comment, one echoed by many others. This results in a high level of connectedness in the parish. If a person is in trouble and does not specifically forbid it, others are told. If there is a need, it is met if possible.

A lot of effort is put into pulling people together at Christ Church. It would be easy in a parish of this size to lose people. Through getting all who wish it involved quickly in appropriate ministries, Christ Church has focused on involvement as a key element in its quest for excellence. They would call this "just being faithful, thank you."

MINISTRY TO THE WHOLE COMMUNITY
• CHURCH OF THE GOOD SHEPHERD

The Church of the Good Shepherd has 160 members serving a community with a year-round population of only 1,200. In theory the parish is four times the size one would expect in such a community. It is a church enthusiastic about their ministry to all the people of Rangeley, and who see this service as vital to their ongoing health.

One aspect of ministry is the use of the church building. The doors are never locked, except the night before some big tag sale or bazaar. The people of Good Shepherd feel this tells the town they welcome people of all types, not just Episcopalians.

If a group needs a place to have their annual dinner, the building is available. The snowmobile club had their annual end-of-season dinner the weekend I visited. Few, if any, members of the parish are part of the club, but they felt it was important to welcome them.

There is a group in the parish hall virtually every night except Monday and often parish committees meet in smaller spaces so that larger non-parish affiliated groups can use the main hall. The parish describes itself as the friendliest in town and is concerned with all that goes on in the community. The town doctor is a member of the parish as is the superintendent of schools, and supporting these people in their work is seen as a part of the ministry of Good Shepherd, too.

This attitude of service extends to the whole community. "If someone is sick or in need people reach out, no matter what church they belong to," said one lay leader. "Works of charity, friendliness, witness and outreach are important here," commented another.

This is especially important in rural Maine where there is a heritage of unfriendliness to outsiders, or people from "away," as they are called. The parish is one of the few places where people who are new to the area will feel welcomed and invited to join in.

"When the chips are down, the parish is there," said one person. "We know that crises will happen to all of us. It might be the death of a much beloved dog or of a grandson; perhaps your kid is getting in trouble. We want to help and we do."

Ministry to the entire community is also embodied in the work of the rector, the Rev. K. Holly Eden. Good Shepherd is the sponsor of the annual high school baccalaureate service. The only other church in town large enough, an independent Baptist church, refuses to host the service because it violates the separation between the secular and the sacred. It was remarkable to me that Holly knew each of the graduates personally and so could really speak to them as they were preparing to leave school.

Another story will further illustrate this ministry. One day Holly Eden received a call from the local police asking her to go and talk to a despondent Vietnam veteran who was holed up in his home. They feared that he might hurt himself or another. "So I went over. He was pretty drunk and he had a lot of guns in the house. I was a little scared but I felt that it was my job to reach out even though I didn't know him. I am not sure if I did any good, but I am always willing to help in a crisis." The man in question did not join the church, but neither was anyone hurt.

Reaching out was seen as a natural part of the ministry of the parish. "I give priority to members of the parish, but in a town like this I am not sure there *is* a difference between the people of the town and the people of the church. We are called to minister to all of them," said the rector. The church continues to be strong while the Roman Catholic and Congregational parishes are cutting back from full-time to part-time clergy. The people of Good Shepherd feel that to a large extent this is because they have never lost sight of the call to minister to the community, both through the use of buildings and person to person contact. I believe that it is partially due to this focus that the Church of the Good Shepherd continues to thrive when others are declining.

SUPPORT OF MISSION THROUGH THE USE OF PHYSICAL AND FINANCIAL RESOURCES
• ST. GEORGE'S

In 1982 St. George's Episcopal Church was literally on the move! The church, for years located in a back alley, was put on a large trailer built for the occasion and moved to a corner location on the main street. This enabled the parish to build a much needed undercroft and to add a parish hall, a space used for overflow on major feast days.

This undertaking absorbed much of the attention of the congregation for several years. Once it was done, the parish leadership felt a new focus for the life of the parish was needed. After much prayer and discussion, the parish chose to use its physical and financial resources to support outside mission work.

A mission committee was established, which was to become the center of much of the life of the parish. It drew some of the best lay leadership and received a lot of support from the clergy staff, especially the rector, the Rev. David Holroyd.

The committee focused on the use of the building. It felt the building should not be kept as just a parish resource but as a community center. To this end, the church sought out groups to use the building and decided to leave it open 24 hours a day as a symbol of the openness of the parish to the community. Head Start, the community chorus, AA, Al-Anon, Weight Watchers, and the local bridge league were all invited in.

This was just the beginning. Three mission projects were also part of the parish strategy. Meals-on-Wheels received a lot of support from the parish with St. George's contributing funds and drivers. Many members became involved with the local hospice program for the terminally ill, and this was seen as having spiritual benefits as well. Finally, the parish made a major commitment to the Emergency Service Project, an organization to help the transients who occasionally become stranded in this resort community.

These are relatively routine activities which,

while important, did not serve to push the people of St. George's significantly beyond themselves. The parish leadership felt this was a beginning, but as they looked around there were simply not too many pressing needs in the immediate area. How could they reach beyond their community?

The answer was in the use of financial resources. York Harbor is an affluent community of retirees, professionals, and people who work in the tourist economy's service sector. Of the lay leaders surveyed, over 70 per cent were professionals or managers of businesses. Their income averaged around $50,000 a year and they each contributed around $2,000 a year to the church. Parish giving as a whole averaged almost $750 per year. It was decided to seek to meet needs outside the parish by financial gifts.

The goal was to move toward a standard of giving away as much as the parish spent on itself. The possibility and challenge of 50-50 giving was raised up by the bishops of the Episcopal Church in 1985, but few parishes saw this as a real possibility. St. George's has accepted it as a parish goal.

In 1987 the parish operating budget was $96,655, really quite small for a parish of this size. This was made possible in part through the use of volunteer secretarial help and a part-time assistant. The parish gave away $26,770, almost

30 per cent of the budget! This is by far the highest percentage given outside the local church in the Diocese of Maine. And the parish is rightly quite proud of the accomplishment. But it sees itself as being in process, not as having completed the task.

Where does the money go? Much of it goes to support the mission and ministry of the Diocese of Maine and of the national Episcopal Church. This is normal and the parish felt that it was unremarkable. But they also support a couple of poor families, one in the south and one in the third world. Reports on these families are made regularly to the parish and in kind help is also given. Other gifts go to special projects as needed. The rector told me that sometimes the bishop of Maine just calls up and asks if the parish can help another church. In one case, a mission in the northern part of the state needed a new roof. The parish was able to contribute. Another time a church in a neighboring state burned down and St. George's was able to give several thousand dollars to help rebuild.

That this mission outside the parish provides the focus for St. George's is revealed in the number of times I heard about it from lay people. People are aware of the call to move toward a 50-50 budget and are supportive of such a move. They are proud of the help they are able to give others and see it as a unique aspect of their ministry. The parish is concerned with worship, Christian education for both adults and children, pastoral care, and the nurturing of the spiritual lives of its people, but it is this focus on mission outside the parish which provides much of the energy which keeps St. George's moving forward.

CONCLUSIONS

It is necessary for a parish to have a focus for its life and ministry in order to be excellent. While all of the parishes in this study are concerned to be balanced in their ministry, in each there is a focus which serves to energize the parish to excel. Because of the complexity of parish life the focus may not be immediately obvious to the casual observer, but upon deeper examination it stands out as the dominant concern in the life of the parish.

The focus is not static; it may change as circumstances change. But it is a dynamic and enlivening spiritual force in the life of a parish. Without a focus a parish may do well but it will not excel.

How is a focus chosen? Is it discerned by the people or does the leadership simply announce it to the people and hope they will follow? It is my belief that in each of these parishes the focus was present in nascent form but that it was the role of the lay and ordained leadership to articulate the vision and to rally the parish to it.

How does this happen? That is the subject of the next section.

Clerical leadership

As I conducted the numerous interviews of lay people and clergy which made up the bulk of this study, the key place of the vicar or rector became an almost constant theme. "We're strong because we reflect the personality of our rector." "Our growth dates from the day he arrived." "He sets the climate and gets people involved and recruited and active." "The minister leads and channels people's energies." "We have a holy priest." "I'm here because of the rector, she is an inspiration." "Why are we excellent? Two words, our rector."

The leadership of the clergy is the *single most important factor in the success of any parish;* not the only factor, but the most important. Strong clergy enable parishes to become strong. Without strong clerical leadership parishes fall apart. Some slowly, some quickly, but they all become unraveled over time.

What does strong clerical leadership look like? From present and past we have several leadership styles, among them the "father knows best" model which was popular in some parishes in the 1950s. In this model the priest was expected to know all and do all with the laity playing docile sheep to the clergyman's (they were all men then) shepherd. Another is the "facilitator," the one who has no opinions, just wants what the people want. A third is of the "therapist/wounded healer," who counsels and helps people find themselves. Another is of the "religious professional," the fully trained graduate of a prestigious divinity school who functions as the skilled practitioner of MINISTRY, an arcane field which is only accessible to the equally trained and dedicated.

There have been many other models, but these are some of the most common. None of them reflects the style of any of the clergy who lead the parishes in this study. All are too limited and inflexible. What happens to the facilitator when he or she needs to take a stand? What happens to the "father" or the therapist when the situation is more than they can handle alone? In each case the model's effectiveness is limited.

The model of leadership which has enabled the six parishes to excel might be called self-differentiated leadership. This model is discussed in depth by Edwin Friedman in his book *Generation to Generation: Family Process in Church and Synagogue* (New York: The Guilford Press, 1985).

Friedman, an ordained rabbi, describes the model in the following way: The leader recognizes his or her place as "head" and works to define his or her own goals and self while staying in touch with the rest of the organization—in this case, the congregation. Though there may be initial resistance to the leader's leading, if the leader can stay in touch with the resisters the congregation will usually follow.

It is vital that the leader be a self while at the same time being part of the congregation. Friedman says this is very difficult, and "Remaining connected becomes increasingly difficult in direct proportion to the leader's success at defining his or her own being."

Another important factor is the leader's capacity and willingness to take nonreactive, clearly conceived, and clearly defined positions. This, says Friedman, "is easier to accomplish in isolation when the leader is not in touch with (or beholden to) the rest of the system."

This style of leadership may feel like a juggling act some of the time but it does serve to move a parish along in a way that no other style does. When the parish leader is willing to take stands *while at the same time holding continued relationship with the parish as a highest personal value*, a powerful synergy develops. On the one hand the parish, an often amorphous collection of people drawn together by the faith but often unsure why, is given a vision toward which they can work, a common goal which will focus common energy. On the other hand, the clergy, an often curmudgeonly and independent group of people, define the vision in terms of what they hear from the parish as to the people's aspirations and visions. And because at root is a common shared value of relationship and mission neither clergy nor laity become absorbed by the other. They both retain their integrity.

This blessed state can only happen if the clergy and the parish are well matched. The pastor-parish relationship in each of the study parishes is unique and alive. One could not randomly substitute one cleric for another and have equal likelihood of success. Yet in each situation the clergy, while sharing many of the values, hopes and dreams of their congregations, are very aware of how they are similar and how they are different from the congregations in their care. The result is that when the congregation itself has difficulty deciding what to do the clergy can often take a stand which enables the rest of the congregation to move out of a deadlock and into motion again.

The need for this kind of action does not come often but when it does the role of the clergy becomes critical. In each of these congregations the clergy, sometimes over and over again, have taken clear stands at crucial times and enabled the congregations to continue to grow. In hindsight it was obvious to all that the clergy were in fact embodying the wishes of the majority of the congregation, but this was not at all clear at the time. On average this kind of stand seems to be needed every four to seven years. It may not seem that only one decision every half-decade is so important, but in the life of these parishes it has been so.

In the remainder of this chapter I will cite examples of strong leadership by the clergy which will generally fall into two categories: Actions which demonstrate staying connected and actions which show the power of self-differentiated leadership. The results of staying connected to a community one likes are: enthusiasm, shared experiences leading to spiritually deep relationships, involvement of the laity, high willingness to be active, and good discernment. The results of being clear about how one feels, of being a "self" are: ability to keep from being absorbed by the congregation, the ability to take the right stand at the right time, an ability to "shift the scales" at a crucial time to enable the congregation to keep moving forward, the joy of being accepted for who one is, and the willingness to take chances in sermons, personal life and congregational life, knowing that things will not always work out as one hopes.

In these congregations the melding of

connectedness and clarity has been a formula for success and faithfulness.

STAYING CONNECTED AND ITS CONSEQUENCES

All of the clergy in this study spend the majority of their time talking with their people. This happens in a variety of settings: home, the supermarket, on the golf course, in meetings, at coffee hour, in counseling sessions of various types, in the hospital, on the street, at the post office, doing service projects, indeed anywhere people might be found. The conversations may be profound or mundane, spiritual or secular, but they all serve to maintain and deepen the connectedness of people and clergy. This aspect of the work of a parish priest does not usually have any particular agenda. It is often very simple yet can be quite deep. It does, however, have definite outcomes.

Respect

One is that as the clergy get to know their people they have more respect for them as persons and more understanding of the spiritual struggles they go through.

The Rev. K. Holly Eden of the Church of the Good Shepherd, Rangeley, Maine, found that the better she knew her people the better she was able to help them. "I come from Central New York. The people here are a lot like the people of New York, but there are some real differences. I cannot minister to them very well if I do not know them." She has found that the question of development of this resort community is one which is very pressing for both the "natives" and the people from "away." "Development affects us all. People here have an affection for the land, yet they need development to boost the economy. And as a result of development people are often working on Sundays. This has an effect on spiritual life as well. They would like to be in church but they cannot. I need to figure out how to respond to that." By staying connected to her people she does not take the absence of a person who works on Sunday as a rejection but rather seeks to find ways to nurture them in the midst of this evolving situation. It is not easy, but the alternative, rejecting them or forcing them to choose between the church and work, is even worse.

Holly has also found that the common sharing of spiritual struggles has strengthened her work in the congregation. When she lost a parent she did not try to hide from the congregation the effect it had on her. The result was an increase in mutual respect. "She let us know about her weakness and her questions and so I was better able to let her minister to me in my weakness," said one lay person. Holly notes that while she does not share everything with the congregation, openness is a powerful model and allows her to lead better.

In this she is like other clergy in this study. They talk freely about their successes and struggles and find that their congregations are willing to follow suit and move deeper in sharing their common journey and struggle to live the faith. "He is so human and I really like that," was a common comment about these clergy.

Enthusiasm

Another result of staying connected is an increase in the enthusiasm the clergy had for their congregations. The Rev. Antoine Campbell of Holy Cross/Faith Memorial spoke about this most eloquently. "They didn't know how wonderful they were. They had been getting poor clergy leadership and mixed messages from the diocese and they needed to know how important they were." He came and told them that they had the power to do great things for a congregation of only 35 people and he found that soon they began to do even better.

This affection increased over time. "The better I get to know them the more I am impressed. They have been strong for years in the face of real problems: indifference from the diocese, small numbers, lack of money, the absence of a priest who cared, a deteriorating economic situation on the island which caused many of their children to leave. And yet they have continued and built one of the strongest ministries anywhere. This is a family-sized church with a corporate-sized ministry."

Increasing enthusiasm over time was common to all of the clergy. "To know them is to love them," said Ladson Mills. "They are just wonderful people," was Gil Birney's comment. "This is a caring, compassionate group of people and we drive each other crazy sometimes," was the affectionate comment of Holly Eden. "If you want to come into a church that loves, come here," was the view of John Frost after 23 years.

I believe this increase in enthusiasm, which grows over time, is an important aspect of the success of the parishes in this study. Churches are voluntary associations and if the most visible leader is happy and upbeat about the community then people will come in. Newcomers often spoke about the positive energy they felt in coming into these parishes, and this is projected by the clergy.

One place where the enthusiasm spills over is in the amount of good humor. People could be serious, but often kidded each other in meetings or at coffee hour. Humorous comments often leavened the announcements from both clergy and laity, and a sense of humor in the clergy was seen by lay people as almost a prerequisite for success. In one parish this was stated as a theological truth. "If you take yourself too seriously then you are not taking the gospel seriously enough," was an often-cited comment of Gil Birney's. People want to be part of a positive experience and the joy of the clergy is infectious in each of these parishes.

Discernment

Because they are so well connected to their people most of the clergy are able to recruit lay people for the tasks of ministry with relative ease. Another way to describe this is to say they are able to use the gift of discernment. This is not only the exercise of good judgment; it is acquiring enough data to make a wise judgment.

In this John Frost is a master. "If you tell John that you are interested in something, fairly soon someone is going to ask you to be part of a group doing just that," said several lay people at Christ Church. Everyone seemed to be involved in something they liked and this is one of the marks of success at Christ Church.

John might be the best at this, but almost

every priest uses this skill to some extent. The story of Gil Birney's altar guild directress is a good example. "I do the altar," she told me. "When I came to this church I had been involved in being altar guild directress in my old parish. I told Gil. A while later he called to ask me if I would organize the altar guild, as St. Bart's didn't have one. I was happy to." St. Bart's does not put a lot of emphasis on having a fancy altar, but this woman was enabled quickly to exercise her gifts because the vicar used his gift of discernment.

None of these parishes has the perpetual volunteer crisis which seems the lot of so many churches. These clergy assume that the gifts are there to enable the congregation to do the work it is called to do. They use the knowledge they get through staying connected to their people to match gifts with appropriate tasks. The result is high levels of both activity and happiness on the part of people, priest and parish.

Spiritual Appropriateness

One of the results of being connected to the lay folk of the parish is an ability on the part of the clergy to lead in a spiritually appropriate way. There is a multitude of spiritual issues present in the world and not all can be covered in any given sermon. In these congregations the clergypersons focus most on the issues with which they find their people struggling.

"If there is a problem which has come up during the week, you can be sure that Gil will talk about it," was a remark I heard. "He always seems to know just what I am thinking about," someone said about David Holroyd. This is not because Father Holroyd is omniscient, but because he is in touch with where his people are. Other parishes echoed this thought.

Because congregations and their settings differ, each clergyperson addresses spiritual issues in a different way. Tony Campbell places a greater emphasis on social justice. John Frost is more family oriented. Ladson Mills finds that responsibility for those who are less fortunate comes out as a theme fairly often. Gil Birney addresses reaching out and drawing people in as a theme with some regularity. The emphasis comes from the focus of each congregation, and the focus emerges because the clergy choose it as the best expression of the gospel call to the community they serve. Without the effort to stay connected to their people this would be impossible.

As congregations grow and change so do the issues with which they struggle. The clergy find that since the context in which they serve is dynamic they must never slack in seeking to remain to touch with their people. If they do, they find they begin to drift apart and so they are less able to lead those in their charge. Some of the clergy have found there were times when because of peculiar circumstances—high stress at home, a series of emergencies demanding a lot of time in the parish, over-involvement in outside activities—they began to lose touch with the congregation. When they perceived this happening, their first priority when the problems subsided was to re-engage as quickly as possible. When they did not, they found their ministry suffered.

SELF-DIFFERENTIATION

It is possible to become too connected with the parish. As Friedman notes, fusion is a common problem among clergy, one leading to a breakdown of the pastor-parish relationship (*Generation to Generation*, p. 231). It is important to remain separate yet connected. In the parishes of this study all of the clergy are respected because of their ability to be clear about who they are as individuals. One aspect of this is the willingness of clergy to let their people see both their strengths and weaknesses. This enabled people to relate to them as people and not just as symbols. John Frost is seen as being very *macho*, "a man's man." This is not appealing to everyone, but he is a former army fighter pilot and it is accepted in him. Holly Eden has a great affection for her dogs. She tells stories about them and it is clear that they are an important part of her life. There are people in her congregation who like her animals and there are some who do not. Because she is clear about where she stands they are free to choose. Yet it is clear that one can stay in close relationship with her and not have to like her pets.

These examples may seem trivial but they do point to an ability to be separate from the people of the congregation. If people can differ on matters of personal style, this opens up the possibility of being able to differ on matters of substance and still remain in relationship.

In all of the parishes studied, the private life of the clergy is allowed to remain as private as they wish. All the clergy spouses are involved in the parish, usually quite actively, but they are allowed to determine what they will and will not do. In this, the proper use of their personal gifts for ministry is held to be the appropriate criteria for activity, as it is for everyone else.

The ability to take a stand

Perhaps the most important by-product of personal self-differentiation is the ability to take stands on crucial parish issues when needed, even when that means alienating some members. Some of the clergy have taken such stands and found that these times were of crucial importance to the life of the parish.

Fairly early on in the Rev. Ladson Mills' ministry at the Church of Our Savior it became clear that the camp chapel in which the congregation had been meeting was inadequate. The church had grown so rapidly that this small space which had once been large enough was now woefully undersized. On many Sundays people were forced to stand outside the doors because there was no room.

The chapel was located at the Diocese of South Carolina's Camp St. Christopher, within the planned community of Seabrook Island. In order for people who lived outside Seabrook to come to church it was necessary to pass through guard gates at the entrance. The guards had been instructed to allow people access to the camp, but it was still necessary to stop and be passed through to get to the church.

The people of Kiawah and Seabrook, who made up 98 per cent of the members of the parish, were used to passing through the gates. When the question of where to locate the new church was brought up, many felt it should be located within the bounds of Seabrook, "where it has always been." Others felt that if the church were truly to be open to all the people of John's

Island, those within Kiawah and Seabrook and those outside, then it should be located outside the gates in a place where all would feel welcome.

This question occasioned considerable debate. In the midst of this the vicar began to realize that the church was called to be the "visible Body of Christ in this community." This meant, he felt, that the building must be located outside the gates, and so he began to state this position. As the debate continued more and more members of the congregation began to agree. Some people felt this was an unimportant matter and others felt quite strongly that the church should be located where the people were, either in Kiawah or Seabrook. As the vicar and the mission council became clearer about locating outside the gates, some people threatened to leave the church if this decision was implemented. This caused a lot of worry on the part of some members. "If the church is meant to include all people, can we act in a way which will force some people out?" Also, the congregation was not yet large enough to be able to lose anyone without serious effects.

Yet the need to be the church in mission and service was one of the elements which had drawn people to the congregation. In the words of one old-timer, "People wanted to just retire here, but soon they got bored. Serving others was important." The church waffled until the vicar pushed the decision to locate outside the gates. They needed, he felt, to decide and get on with the task of building.

It was a watershed event. Some people did leave. Over time some came back and some stayed away. But through the clarity of Ladson's position on this issue, the parish was saved from being primarily inwardly directed, and instead became the vibrant, mission-oriented place it now is. The symbolism of being outside the controlled communities was not lost on the people of the island, and they have felt much more connected to the people of the Church of Our Savior ever since.

Ladson Mills is not the only cleric in charge to make this kind of a decision, although this is perhaps the most dramatic case. Every one of the clergy in this study has had to take a clear stand on some crucial issue in the life of the congregation in order to keep the community moving forward on its journey. In fact it seems that these decisions come fairly regularly.

The Rev. John Frost told of several decisions. Soon after he arrived at Christ Church with the mandate from the bishop to keep the parish from getting further in debt, he spent $70,000 on a new parish hall because they needed it. He led the church to focus on different areas of ministry over the years, first families and children, then growth and the construction of new buildings, and then fellowship and strengthening community. Each of these was a theme for about seven years, then a new focus would emerge. The rector was the key person in the making of each of these decisions and without his leadership the parish might have faltered.

The Rev. David Holroyd said moving the church and deciding to focus on outreach were both crucial decisions in his ministry. For Gil Birney it was the realization that incorporation of newcomers was the great gift of St. Bart's. Tony Campbell's crucial decision was to help Holy Cross/Faith Memorial be the "soul" of Episcopal Outreach of Pawley's Island. In each case the clergy were called to take stands on issues and then the parish followed.

The ability of the clergy to know when to take a stand and then to use their full authority to do it is one of the key characteristics of the leadership of excellent parishes. Through staying connected the clergy remain aware of the feelings of the congregation about a particular issue, but it is the ability to discern the critical nature of an issue and then to take a stand which is their outstanding gift. In the vivid but gory phrasing of Ladson Mills, a former Marine officer, "You have to know which trenches are worth dying in."

All of these clergy do.

The stands taken do not concern a single transient decision. Rather they concern key long term issues such as locating a church, and may take years to resolve. But they do get resolved.

THE QUESTION OF LONGEVITY

The pastors who participated in this study have been in their parishes for varying lengths of time. The Rev. Tony Campbell has been in place the shortest, just under four years, and John Frost has been at Christ Church for the past 23 years. One of the long term contributions of the clergy is the recruitment of strong lay people who then enable the parish to grow in strength. Holy Cross/Faith Memorial, with its unique demographic situation, is the exception. In every other congregation many of the key lay people who make the congregation what it is today have become active in the congregation because of the leadership of the present clergy.

Christ Church was a struggling mission with fewer that 100 people 23 years ago. It now has over 680 and most of them will cite the ministry of John Frost as the reason they have come and stayed. He said there were many times when he wondered if the whole situation was unredeemable and would collapse. But he said he just tried to be faithful day by day and this turned into year by year. The result was not dramatic growth but a slow, steady increase which has now resulted in Christ Church being one of the largest parishes in the diocese. As one lay leader said, "These are the good times. Times were not always good and John Frost's faithfulness has enabled us to come to this point."

The Church of Our Savior has grown from 50 families to 150 in eight years, St. Bartholomew's has quadrupled in size. In each of these situations the excellent preaching and teaching of the clergy, their style of pastoral care and their leadership on important issues were cited over and over by lay people as the reasons for being a part of the parish. While St. Bart's may seem to have grown overnight, to its people this has felt like a long process. At the Church of Our Savior there is a real sense that their current size was not "foreordained by God" but was rather the result of patient labor on the part of clergy and lay people.

The key role of the clergy is even more dramatically underscored by the example of the Church of the Good Shepherd. This parish has been relatively stable in size, but is increasing in the ministry it performs largely because of the quality of the lay leadership. This leadership has entered the parish because of the clergy. The only doctor in Rangeley settled in that town partially because of the strength of the Episcopal Church there. Many of the community leaders who attend say it is a place of spiritual, not political, nurture for them. The volunteer director of religious education of the local Congregational church left there because of conflict and found herself drawn to Good Shepherd because of Holly Eden. This has enabled the parish to strengthen its Christian education program and to begin to draw in new families with children.

The need for patience cannot be stressed too highly. While these six parishes may seem to outsiders to be growing rapidly, to those on the inside the process seems slow and sometimes tedious. "It may seem exciting, but it just seems like work to me most of the time," said Ladson Mills, a comment echoed in one form or another by all of the clergy. They work hard and patiently and over time their work bears fruit, but there are no quick fixes.

CONCLUSIONS

When asked by a lay person what single act was most critical for the success of a parish, my response was "get the best clergy person you can." When asked what the role of the clergy was, lay person after lay person noted that "the rector sets the tone" and that it is in a climate of holy reflection, faithful prayer, mature community, and quality pastoral care that they find what they are looking for. I believe that strong clergy enable and perhaps produce strong parishes. Strong does not mean tyrannical. Strength in this case means being self-differentiated, willing to lead by taking stands when necessary, but at the same time staying connected to the community of faith. These two positions are in tension, but if one can hold them in a kind of dynamic balance the results are superb.

The results can be seen in the six study parishes. They make the correct major decisions, they sense the difference between the trivial and the crucial. Lay leaders who want to be part of a strong parish join these and enable them to become even stronger and better able to minister to one another and the world. Without strong clerical leadership a parish will falter. With strong leadership by the clergy the parish will grow, but it will take time. Over time the parish will become a powerhouse of ministry, largely executed and led by the laity.

Lay leadership

Strong clergy leadership is important. So is strong lay leadership. It may seem to some that these are mutually exclusive. Stories of lay/clergy conflict can be heard in many gatherings of church leaders. After all, how can there be two different power centers? It would seem inevitable that the two would come into conflict and that a profound loss of effectiveness would result. This has not been the case in the six congregations of this study. Strong clergy and strong laity go together. Indeed, strong clergy seem to draw strong laity. They support one another.

This is borne out by the levels of lay involvement in the study parishes. In each congregation the levels of lay activity are extraordinary. Besides the leadership of the elected vestry members, leadership is also exercised by   people in every phase of congregational life.

Any church will be active in too many areas of ministry for an individual to manage and lead them all. This necessitates a choice for the designated leader, in this case the professional clergy person in charge. She or he may either choose to limit the activity of the congregation to a level one person can manage, or choose to delegate and empower others to assist in the

105

work of the parish. In every church in this study it is the latter course which is followed.

But leadership of the laity also grows out of another phenomenon. This is the desire of lay people to exercise their gifts for ministry in concrete and validated ways. They do not only act when the clergy ask them but take responsibility for leadership of new projects. At Holy Cross/ Faith Memorial it was the lay people who initiated and then recruited children for a church school program. At the Church of Our Savior lay people started a tutoring program for students at the public high school. While this would not have been possible without the tacit support of the clergy, neither was active clerical leadership needed.

The desire of the laity to lead grows out of a belief shared by clergy and laity that God has called the whole community of the parish to ministry. Rather than worry that the parish will be spread too thin by the multiplying of calls to specific ministry, all of the clergy assume God has given the parish all the gifts needed for its work. If the task is not ordained to succeed it will fail. Because the clergy know God has not deposited all the gifts in an individual, they are also clear that the success or failure of all projects does not rest with them. All ministry becomes a cooperative venture drawing upon the wisdom, energy, enthusiasm and spirituality of both laity and clergy. The result is a *community* engaged in ministry. This cooperative stance has some definite effects.

IDEA GENERATORS

A key role of the lay leadership is that of idea generators. "Anyone can suggest anything and it will be considered," was a comment about St. George's. "We're good at taking risks, and so people are encouraged to speak up," I heard at St. Bart's. "Sometimes it works and sometimes it doesn't, but if you don't try, nothing will happen," a member of Holy Cross/Faith Memorial commented.

This attitude fosters a climate of experimentation. Because there is excitement about the future in all of these parishes, the willingness to try new things is also present. Not everything works out. There are often failures of new ideas. But most of the time they succeed.

No parish in the study plans longer in advance than one year. The general attitude is that life changes so much in a year that no one can predict beyond that. The result is an institution of one-year plans formed through the use of an annual vestry conference. The parish uses the experience of the past year to plan for the next.

Ideas can and do come from anywhere; there is no stagnation. New events happen all the time.

ANYONE CAN LEAD

The questionnaire's statement, "Every member has an equal opportunity to hold key leadership positions," met with moderate to strong agreement in every parish. One of the characteristics of the congregations in the study is a desire to let people become as involved as they wish. And one of the desires of the people, it became clear upon interviewing both lay leaders and others, is to be involved in the leadership of the church.

In most parishes the primary decisions are made by the elected lay leadership and the rector. But this is not exclusively so. The circle of decision makers is as wide as the ministry of the parish. People who are involved in church school make decisions relating to that, the worship committees focus on worship, the choir helps to decide what music they will sing, the building and property committees make decisions with regard to those areas. In a denomination with what is considered a relatively hierarchical polity the spread of decision making among many people is remarkable.

This leads to a feeling that major decisions

are not in the hands of just a few people. Rather, anyone can participate if they wish to do so, and are willing to work with others toward consensus. No one, including the clergy, is allowed to dictate; everyone is expected to participate.

An example of this was the beginning of the imaginative church school program at Holy Cross/ Faith Memorial, bringing in children from the community. A few of the lay people got together and developed a plan for using the church's mini-vans to transport children, with or without their parents, to church on Sundays for worship and teaching. The vicar, the Rev. Antoine Campbell, was opposed at first. He felt that they could be spread too thin by this ministry. But the people of the parish were clear in wanting to exercise this ministry. The vicar decided he was in the way and withdrew opposition, but neither did he actively support this project. Within a year the church school was up to over twenty students and was a success. The ministry went forward because of a shared sense that God can call anyone to leadership and mission, not just the clergy. This kind of story can be told of almost any of the congregations.

SELF-DIFFERENTIATED LAY LEADERSHIP

The initiation of a mission activity by one

person or a group does not lead to a lot of withdrawal by those who are "defeated" in the process of making the decision. The reason is that the lay leadership, as well as the clergy leadership, practices a style similar to Friedman's theory of self-differentiation; that is, knowing yourself and holding the desire to do what is best for the community as a highest personal value. People know how to take a stand, but since everyone attempts to live the value of remaining in relationship with one another, the needs of the community are held above personal desires.

One person at St. George's in York Harbor stated that as a result "people are not always happy, but they are at peace." This allows people to exercise leadership in areas where they are skilled and to allow others to do the same in other areas. The people who like to cook food are not required to enjoy accounting, the people who teach church school do not have to enjoy being with the elderly. People are honored for what they do and given space not to do everything. The individual gifts of the members of the church are thus affirmed and people are empowered to do their individual mission and ministry within the context of the whole community. The result is a climate of non-competitive activity for mission and ministry. This allows many different areas of ministry which work cooperatively to move the whole community forward.

COMMUNITY LEADERS BECOME PARISH LEADERS

One phenomenon I observed was that people who are leaders in the community are also leaders in the church. People who lead in one place in their lives seem to be drawn to Christian communities where they are encouraged to lead as well. At the Church of the Good Shepherd in Rangeley, Maine, the town physician, the school superintendent and a number of local leaders were present. They led in the community outside church and saw leadership within the church as appropriate as well. At Holy Cross/Faith Memorial the lay leadership of the parish was often involved in community projects outside the parish, such as an African-American Heritage Festival. At Christ Church, Peachtree, many of the state college faculty and other community leaders were a part of the parish. All felt that they would have left if they had not been encouraged to lead. At the Church of Our Savior many of the members had been leaders in community, business and industry. While they were not currently leaders in the local community, they had been.

CONSENSUS, HARMONY AND LOW RATES OF BURNOUT

The people of the Church of Our Savior modeled cooperation with a maturity they said resulted from the high number of retirees present. The kind of people who could pick up and move to coastal South Carolina would be among the best of society, they felt. These people who had been decision makers in the past would know that you can't win every time, and so would be gracious. This level of self-knowledge was common in every parish.

There is a definite desire to work together within the lay leadership of these parishes. Occasionally one will hear a story of a lone wolf, but most of the time people are interested in what other people are doing and as far as possible supportive of it. If they do not agree, they may argue against it until the decision is made but once a course of action is decided upon even passive resistance ceases.

I believe this attitude is rooted in the Christian faith which is so well taught by the clergy of the study parishes. When one is trying to build Christian community, one is willing to surrender some personal autonomy for the benefit of the community. The values of service, mutual support and common mission in the name of Jesus Christ are practiced as well as taught.

One result of low conflict and affirmation of the particularity of gifts and of leadership by anyone, is that there is little lay leader burnout. Because people are free to find their own avenues of work within the parish community they tend to work hard at tasks they enjoy. The result is a combination of very hard work, excitement and wide dispersion of tasks. No one is essential, including the clergy, but all are valued. This leads to low levels of guilt when circumstances necessitate a change in intensity of activity on the part of lay people. Workers can slack off when they need to because there is always an abundance of people to do the tasks of the parish. This also allows people who have had to slow down to re-engage if and when they want to.

NEW MEMBER RECRUITERS AND ENTHUSIASTS

The final role which the laity play in all of these parishes is that of evangelists. Over 80 per cent had invited someone to church in the past year and almost 70 per cent had invited two or more families to become part of the congregation in that time. This is a high average and led to the significant growth rates of some of the congregations.

Such evangelism comes out of a positive

feeling about the church. Over 90 per cent of the people surveyed had moderate or strongly positive feelings about their parishes and about the future of the parish. When asked if they thought their parish was excellent most people wondered what that meant. When asked if they would tell a friend that the church was an excellent one that they would enjoy being part of, almost everyone answered "yes!" The first question seemed to relate to some abstract ideal standard while the second was more down to earth. They knew they were part of fine churches.

This enthusiasm has other corollaries. It enables these parishes to function with a minimum of fuss most of the time. Energy does not get siphoned off into a lot of "poor us" negativity. Rather, energy is channeled into seeking to be the most faithful Christian communities they can be and trying different ways to achieve that. Many ideas work. Not all do. If something fails, they try to learn from that and then move on. It produces an excitement which is palpable.

CONCLUSION

It would be a big mistake to see the church as consisting of clergy leaders and lay followers. The role of the clergy is crucial but very specific. In all the study parishes much of the leadership and almost all of the work is done by lay people. They are encouraged to generate ideas and to follow through on inspirations which sometimes succeed and sometimes fail.

The commonly shared value of doing Christ's work in the world while remaining in community is central to this. Both lay and clerical leadership have high threat thresholds. They can allow people to be different because they know who they themselves are.

It is appropriate that there are high levels of lay leadership and activity in these parishes. After all, the laity are the arms and hands of Christ in the world and it is through the *laos* that the mission of the church is accomplished, to reconcile all people to one another and God in Christ.

Conclusions

The parishes which were the subject of this study are excellent by almost any broad-based standard. The criteria which the bishops and their staffs used to select the churches were limited in scope (high levels of lay ministry, outperforming the demographics of the area, strong stewardship) and led to parishes which are models of the faithful communities most churches would like to be. The parishes are not without fault—that is not excellence but fantasy—but they are living the full life of mission activity, worship and education which most parishes aspire to.

The objective criteria support the notion that faithfulness will produce strength. Even tiny Holy Cross/Faith Memorial has had dramatic increases in per person giving during the ministry of Tony Campbell. All the parishes have significantly outperformed the demographics of their areas, either growing faster than the surrounding communities in numbers and in dollar support or maintaining strength in the face of a declining situation. Yet none of these church communities set out to build up numbers; they set out to be faithful. The good news is that faithfulness will bring tangible rewards; not overnight but over time.

It is worth noting that there were urban parishes in the two dioceses, but none of them were selected by their bishops as "excellent." I feel comfortable that the conclusions of this study will apply not only to most rural, town and suburban parishes but to urban parishes as well, and that certainly there are excellent urban parishes.

There are five keys to the success of the study parishes.

First: The faith is taught from the pulpit. The preaching of short, simple sermons which come out of the scripture and apply to the daily lives of the people of the parish is central to the success of these churches. The need for this cannot be overemphasized! If the people of the community are bored with what they hear on Sundays, if they are not inspired to reflection on a regular basis, then the parish will not thrive.

Second: The whole parish strives to live out the reality of being the community of faith. This comes out in the high levels of mutual support given one another in times of crisis, in high levels of interpersonal sharing in both formal and informal settings, and in the maturity with which people deal with one another. These parishes have disagreements but they do not evolve into the killing conflicts which so bedevil many

Christian communities. People hold remaining in relationship with one another as a highest value, and the result is that they can truly struggle with questions of what it means to be faithful, knowing that a strong difference of opinion on this matter will not result in a conflict which will divide and possibly harm the parish. This enables these communities to take calculated risks which in turn enables them to grow and learn from both their successes and their failures.

Third: Each parish has sought to find a unique and specific focus for its life and ministry. This focus, while not overwhelming all other tasks of the community of faith, becomes a rallying point for parish energy and creativity. It also keeps the parish moving forward. The focus shifts over time and for short periods of time, usually less than a year, there may be a time of transition, but a focus is always there. The focus emerges out of a combination of the parish's unique situation and the mandates of the gospel as perceived by the leadership of the congregation, both lay and ordained. The emergence of the focus is almost organic, and once identified it becomes central to the parish's ministry and identity.

Fourth: The self-differentiated leadership of the clergy is perhaps the most critical and difficult key. The leadership of clergy who both know themselves and their beliefs and who hold remaining in touch with and in service to their people as a primary aim is central to success. Even in the smallest communities the leadership of the clergy not only in preaching but in day to day life is crucial. In order to be truly excellent the parishes need to be led by clergy who know when to take a stand and when to relax, who can reveal themselves both in strength and weakness to their people, and who spend much if not most of their time keeping in touch with the laity. This stance must be one which comes out of the heart and not out of a book. If one does not truly love the people of one's parish then the parish will never achieve excellence. At the same time if one is unable to be a "self" in the face of the demands of the people of the community then one will be unable to lead at all. As Friedman says, it is the most difficult thing in the world to do, to remain separate yet in relationship. All of these clergy have done this and through this style have been enabled truly to lead their parishes beyond what would normally be expected.

Fifth: Self-differentiated lay leadership. Strong clergy are not enough. They must be matched by strong lay leadership. The people *are* the church and the role of the laity is central. It may seem that this book overemphasizes the contribution of the clergy. It is true that I believe that parishes with poor clergy cannot thrive, but the lay people must be able to speak their minds, and be committed to remaining connected to one another and to discerning the particular mission of the local church. Not everyone will be able to do this, but in the parishes of this study I believe that most of the lay leadership led self-differentiated lives as did their clergy models, and so were able to do the work of the church with a minimum of friction and a maximum of success. I believe strong self-differentiated clergy will draw and nurture strong self-differentiated laity. If one were to ask which comes first I would say usually, but not always, clerical leadership. Yet in some cases, St. Bart's and Holy Cross/Faith Memorial, for example, it is a strong core of lay leaders who influence the clergy, and the two feed each other from there. The exact nature of this process is complex and beyond resolution on the basis of the data from this study.

Where there is excellence in ministry by the whole community I believe that these five factors will be found. I have a lot of confidence in these conclusions because of the breadth and depth of this study. The parishes ranged greatly in size and budget. There were black parishes and white parishes and integrated parishes. Some served the whole community, some served a part of their local populations. They were geographically diverse, upcountry agricultural communities, resorts, retirement, mountain and suburban. They had many different theological and liturgical styles ranging from social activist liberal to very conservative traditionalist. Since such a diverse sample had such high levels of unanimity, I believe the conclusions may have near universal applicability.

If you who are reading this wish to apply the insights of this study in your own parish to make it stronger, what should be done? I believe that there are different tasks for clergy and laity in this process of moving toward excellence and that they relate to the five conclusions outlined above.

For the clergy the first task is to develop a knowledge of self. One cannot practice a self-differentiated leadership style if one does not know oneself. In the case of the clergy in this study, the task of acquiring self-knowledge has taken many different forms. Some emerged from strong families where they were enabled by their parents and siblings to know themselves and were so given a foundation on which to build. For others it was a career before entering the ordained ministry which enabled clarity. For still a third group psychotherapy after entering the ranks of the ordained was needed to develop this clear sense of selfhood. The route is less important than the end. Self-knowledge enables one to distinguish between those issues which are personally important and those which are less so. Such knowledge enables a clergyperson to lead a parish while allowing others to agree or disagree when necessary.

One of the crucial duties of the clergyperson is enabling the community to be as faithful as it can be. If in the process of discovering oneself it becomes clear that one truly does not care for the people being served, it is time to move on or find another way to express one's God-given gifts for ministry. If one finds that one truly does love the people whom he or she is called to serve, but lacks an understanding of what they desire, the next task is to listen to the people and to seek to understand their spiritual needs both as individuals and as a community. This can only emerge through a process of patient listening in all sorts of places: church, home, hospital and street. It will take time but no one else can do it for the ordained leadership.

Once these two tasks are well under way the clergy will find relationships are developing and that the understanding which is acquired will provide a foundation upon which to build a preaching ministry which is vital to the continued strength of the parish. The sermons need to be short and to the point, and more important, connected to people's lives. If this can be done with some consistency then the people of the parish will invite others to share in the personal growth in faith which will emerge, and the parish will grow.

Only when these have been done will the cleric be established as leader of the parish. Parishes need strong leadership. Taking the right stands at the right time can be learned, but it will take time. The proper discernment will come from conversations and self-knowledge. Once this is achieved, the parish can continue to move.

Lest anyone think I believe that this process is simple or quick, I would like to say that it is my observation that it takes at least three years and possibly five before a priest can truly have the authority necessary to be a community's leader. It takes time to learn and develop a strong relationship.

For the laity, I believe the issues are somewhat different but related. Lay people also need to develop the skills of self-differentiation. Lay people need to own their own competence and wisdom and participate in the process of discerning the mission and focus of the parish. Once this has been determined it is the task of the laity to live out that mission. The commitment of people to this process will manifest itself in the life of the parish and will be obvious to any who visit.

If a congregation has a clergyperson who seems unable to lead, they need to deal with the situation, keeping always in mind the basic Christian value of maintaining and building community. If, in the process, relationships are damaged beyond repair then neither the parish nor the Lord will be well served.

A parish in the calling process needs to seek someone who embodies the virtues of self-differentiated leadership as described in this book. But this alone is not enough. A good match between pastor and people in attitudes and values is necessary. I am certain that strong clergy draw strong laity. The reverse is, I believe, also true.

In both dioceses there were several other parishes which could have been selected as subjects for this study. I believe they would have followed the same general pattern. Our Lord has promised us that the gifts will be there if we seek them, and we need to attend primarily to the basic tasks of ministry. Preach the gospel. Be the community of faith. Act boldly to fulfill a unique mission in a particular situation. If we do this we will thrive and bring closer the kingdom of God.

O God of unchangeable power and eternal light: Look favorably on your whole Church, that wonderful and sacred mystery; by the effectual working of your providence, carry out in tranquility the plan of salvation; let the whole world know that things which were cast down are being raised up and things which had grown old are being made new, and that all things are being brought to their perfection by him through whom all things were made, your Son Jesus Christ our Lord; who lives and reigns with you in the unity of the Holy Spirit, on God, for ever and ever. Amen. (BCP, p.540)

Table of Contents

Outline of Joshua, Judges, and Ruth

Joshua

I. The Conquest of Canaan (1:1–12:24)
   A. Preparations (1:1–2:24)
      1. Joshua assumes command (1:1-11)
      2. The Transjordan tribes pledge aid (1:12-18)
      3. The spies (2:1-24)
   B. Crossing the Jordan (3:1–5:15)
      1. God promises help (3:1-13)
      2. The crossing (3:14–4:8)
      3. The crossing completed (4:9-5:1)
      4. In camp at Gilgal (5:2-15)
   C. Attacks on Jericho and Ai (6:1–8:35)
      1. Preparations (6:1-7)
      2. The fall of Jericho (6:8-21)
      3. Rahab spared (6:22-27)
      4. First attack on Ai fails (7:1-26)
      5. Victory at Ai (8:1-35)
   D. Continued conquest (9:1-12:24)
      1. Treaty with Gibeonites (9:1-27)
      2. Southern campaigns (10:1-43)
      3. Northern campaigns (11:1-23)
      4. Conclusion (12:1-24)
II. After the Conquest (13:1–24:33)
   A. Distribution of the land (13:1–21:45)
      1. Land still unconquered (13:1-7)
      2. Inheritance of the Transjordan Tribes (13:8-33)
      3. Division Among Remaining Tribes (14:1–19:51)
      4. Special cities and conclusion (20:1–21:45)

B. Joshua's last days (22:1–24:33)
   1. Departure of Transjordan tribes (22:1-34)
   2. Farewell address (23:1-16)
   3. Covenant at Shechem (24:1-28)
   4. Three burials (24:29-33)

Judges

I. Review of the Conquest (1:1–3:6)
   A. Conquest and settlement (1:1–2:5)
      1. Many a battle (1:1-36)
      2. Departure from Gilgal (2:1-5)
   B. Introduction to the Judges (2:6–3:6)
      1. Joshua dies (2:6-10)
      2. Israel's infidelity (2:11-23)
      3. Israel among the nations (3:1-6)
II. Stories of the Judges (3:7–16:31)
   A. Three early Judges (3:7-31)
      1. Othniel (3:7-11)
      2. Ehud (3:12-30)
      3. Shamgar (3:31)
   B. Deborah and Barak (4:1–5:31)
      1. The oppression (4:1-3)
      2. Deborah and Barak plan (4:4-9)
      3. The victory (4:10-24)
      4. The song of Deborah (5:1-31)

C. Gideon (6:1–8:35)
  1. Problems with the Midianites (6:1-6)
  2. Gideon's call (6:7-32)
  3. Invasion and uncertainty (6:33-40)
  4. Preparations (7:1-15)
  5. Attack and victory (7:16–8:21)
  6. The story ends (8:22-35)
D. Abimelech (9:1-57)
  1. King of Shechem (9:1-6)
  2. Jotham's fable (9:7-21)
  3. Quarrel and rebellion (9:22-41)
  4. The outcome (9:42-57)
E. Six lesser-known Judges (10:1–12:15)
  1. Tola and Jair (10:1-5)
  2. Jephthah (10:6–12:7)
  3. Ibzan and Elon (12:8-12)
  4. Abdon (12:13-15)
F. Samson (13:1–16:31)
  1. The story begins (13:1-25)
  2. A stormy marriage (14:1–15:8)
  3. Confrontation with the Philistines (15:9-20)
  4. Temptations, defeat, and victory (16:1-31)
III. Other Stories (17:1–21:25)
A. The Danites relocate (17:1–18:31)
  1. Micah's story (17:1-13)
  2. The Danites' move (18:1-13)
  3. The Danites and Micah clash (18:14-26)
  4. Settlement at Laish (18:27-31)
B. Gibeah's offense (19:1–21:25)
  1. The Levite's story (19:1-30)
  2. Israel's response (20:1-48)
  3. Making peace again (21:1-25)

Ruth

I. Problem and Initial Solution (1:1–2:23)
   A. Moab (1:1-18)
   B. Bethlehem (1:19-22)
   C. Gleaning (2:1-23)
II. A Happy Ending (3:1–4:22)
   A. Naomi's plan (3:1-18)
   B. A slight hitch (4:1-12)
   C. Conclusion (4:13-22)

Introduction to Joshua

The sixth book of our Bible is named for Joshua, the central figure in its story. That story is the story of Israel's conquest of Canaan. Joshua is a great leader in these events, yet he is not a hero in the usual sense. Joshua does not accomplish great deeds by his own ability. Instead, Joshua appears as God's instrument. It is God who is the real hero here.

Jews have traditionally classed Joshua as the first of the books called the Former Prophets (Joshua–Second Kings). These are not prophetic books as we know them, but they received the name for two reasons: (1) After a time, people began to call all great religious leaders *prophets*, and (2) these books reflect a prophetic view of history.

Christians, on the other hand, usually class Joshua as a historical book, because Joshua tells the history of Israel's conquest and settlement of the Promised Land. More than that, though, this book tells of God's action in and through specific historical events. Joshua gives us both history and a religious interpretation of that history.

Relationship to Other Biblical Books

The Book of Joshua stands as an essential part of the whole historical sequence sweeping from Genesis to Nehemiah. As one portion of the ongoing story of God's action in Israel's history, Joshua has strong ties to many biblical books. In Joshua we see God's fulfillment of the Genesis promises to Abraham. Joshua carries forth the

themes of law and covenant so basic to the Book of
Exodus. Sometimes the man Joshua even appears as a
parallel to the Exodus leader, Moses. The Psalms often
mention the conquest story in poetic praise of God for
mighty acts. As mentioned before, Joshua shares a
religious viewpoint with many of the prophets. The book
has its closest ties, however, with a literary unit that runs
from Deuteronomy through Second Kings. Style and
theology show that this whole epic was probably written
by one school of writers who maintained a standard
outlook and formula for expression. So, Joshua does not
stand alone; it is part of a much larger biblical picture.

Authorship

Literary and theological evidence shows that someone
(probably just one person) from the Deuteronomy–Second
Kings school composed the final version of Joshua. We do
not know this author's name. Instead, for convenience, we
usually call any writer from this school "D," and say
Joshua was written by D. It's not quite that simple,
however. The book is now a well-organized whole, but
there are signs that the author used many older sources for
his work. He has blended together many stories, some of
them ancient tribal traditions whose originators are
unknown. This blending has left a few contradictions. For
instance in 4:8, twelve stones are carried out of the Jordan.
But in 4:9, twelve stones are set up in the river. Either
way, the writer still makes his point. His concern to glorify
God comes through.

Theology

The Book of Joshua shows us a God of unlimited
power, justice, and grace. God acts in historical events of
this world. Israel is God's chosen instrument in the
world. Obedience to God's command gives Israel success;
disobedience brings failure. God's promises are true and
worthy of trust. The covenant is both God's gracious gift

and Israel's moral responsibility.

For special reasons, God wants Israel to possess the land of Canaan. God has promised it and works with the faithful people to bring this about. The conquest is thus a gift, not Joshua's nor Israel's achievement. God's will for the people is freedom and self-determination, and God follows through to give Israel a homeland.

Most of us probably find little quarrel with such a theology. Yet underneath there are some problems. One has been the over-simplification of the "obedience equals success" theory. Some have taken this belief to mean that (1) we can win God's favor by good works, or (2) that every misfortune is proof of sin. Seeing these problems, many have supposed that the writer was a shallow thinker. Perhaps he had not even considered the problem of innocent suffering. So they have written him off. But perhaps the writer was speaking only of the nation's long-term well-being, not of individual short-term events.

Another problem that often bothers readers of Joshua is the picture they see of God as a God of violence and bloodshed, a God who seems to advocate pure mayhem if it suits the divine purposes. Since this is not the God we know through Jesus, many simply dismiss Joshua as primitive religious fanaticism. Others suggest that Israel's religious understanding had just not developed far enough to see God as a God of consistent love toward everyone. But we must remember that peace was always offered before a town was destroyed. The writer may actually be expressing a much deeper thought: that this God is one who works through the people and institutions of this world as they are, good or evil. God uses war, even though it is evil, because God works with what is here, not what we might wish were here.

Dates

In Joshua there are two dates to consider: the date of the events and the date when the writer wrote them down.

The date of the events themselves is fairly clear. After the Exodus from Egypt and the wilderness wanderings, Israel finally established a home in Canaan. This probably happened in the late thirteenth century B.C.

The date of writing is more complex. We cannot tell how old the ancient sources may be. Scholars are fairly sure, however, that the final writing took place in the sixth or seventh century B.C. Most place it during the Exile (587–538 B.C.). Some commentators place the writing just before the fall of Jerusalem in 587 B.C. In either case we find that someone living 600 to 700 years after the event has determined to tie this story together, to preserve his nation's history, and to interpret that history in the light of faith.

Historical Value

With such a time lapse between the events and the final book we might expect some information gaps, some fuzziness on details. And we do find them in Joshua. So how much historical fact can we expect from this book? Our answer, given the circumstances, is: a surprising amount. Because of information from Judges 1 and other sources, scholars formerly thought that the conquest was really a slow infiltration, with each tribe working more or less alone. Some tribes may not even have left Canaan for Egypt at all. This is very different from the concentrated campaigns we see in Joshua. So scholars supposed that Joshua was a idealized version of the process. More recent archeological evidence, however, has shown a massive destruction of Canaanite cites in the thirteenth century. It appears that a concerted effort may have occurred and that Joshua may well be more accurate than previously assumed. For now, we cannot know exactly how quickly or how closely the tribes worked. That need not, however, keep us from understanding the author's main point: the saving, freeing action of God in the history of a faithful, obedient people.

Joshua 1–2

Introduction to These Chapters

From the very first verse the author makes it clear that
the Book of Joshua is a continuation of Israel's great
historical narrative. He takes up precisely where the Book
of Deuteronomy ends, with the death of Moses. Moses
has led the people to God's promised land. Now the
conquest of that land is about to begin.

In the same first verse the author brings in the name of
Joshua. Joshua is to take up where Moses left off. Here
and in the following ten verses is the author's
introduction. It is an introduction that assures a smooth
transition from the last book to this one. In it the author
shows that human leadership is changing, but God's
purposes and position of command are not.

Following the introduction we find some ancient
traditions concerning the conquest itself, including the
story of a specific incident through which God worked to
help Israel toward its first victory. Throughout these
verses, as throughout the book, God is at the center. It is
God who promises, commands, and aids the people.
Joshua is God's instrument for the task at hand.

Here is an outline of these chapters.

I. Joshua Assumes Command (1:1-11)
II. The Transjordan Tribes Pledge Aid (1:12-18)
III. The Spies (2:1-24)

Joshua Assumes Command (1:1-11)

After their escape from Egypt, the Israelites had
wandered in the wilderness (or desert) areas south of
Palestine, waiting for the time when they could enter the
Promised Land. This Promised Land was the land of
Canaan, or Palestine. It lay on the land bridge between
Asia and Africa. The area is split north to south by the
Jordan River. To the east of the Jordan is a plateau. To
the west there is a central mountain range running north
and south, then some foothills, and finally a plain that
continues west to the Mediterranean Sea. (See the map
on page 155.) The people of Israel have come around
Canaan's southern borders to the east bank of the Jordan.
Across the river lies the bulk of their Promised Land. But
it is already occupied. They will have to conquer the
land.

They have come at a good time, however. The Hittite
empire that previously controlled the area has crumbled.
Canaan's towns are not effectively joined or systematically
defended.

Israel's leader, Moses, has died. The mantle of
leadership passes to his assistant, Joshua. It is Joshua
who will now serve as God's instrument to fulfill the
promise of a homeland. God gives instruction and
encouragement. Then Joshua commands the people to
prepare for the invasion.

Joshua means *Yahweh (God) is salvation.* Joshua is
sometimes called *Hoshea* instead. This is the same Joshua
who assisted Moses in the wilderness and who went with
the twelve spies into Canaan (Numbers 13:8; 14:6, 38). Of
those twelve only Joshua and Caleb believed that the land
could be conquered.

Nun is Joshua's father. Nothing is known of Nun
except that he was a member of the tribe of Ephraim.
Some scholars believe that Nun was actually a sub-tribe
rather than an individual.

Minister here is a lieutenant or aide.

Lebanon is the range of mountains to the north of Palestine. The *Euphrates* is a river far to the northeast, and the *great sea* is the Mediterranean.

The *Hittites* were a people from the north who had built a large empire that included much of Palestine. Some Hittites probably still lived in the area, and the old empire was still called the land of the Hittites.

The boundaries of the Promised Land (verse 4) included a territory much larger than any that Israel ever actually controlled. They reflect, however, the hope that Israel would someday be a large, strong nation.

God offers strength on condition that the people be steadfast, remain faithful, and take care to obey the *Book of the Law* (verse 8). This book is evidently the law as written in the Book of Deuteronomy. Here we see the writer's special concern with this law.

The Jordan River split Palestine north to south. Israel was camped on the east side of the Jordan. Most of the Promised Land lay west of the Jordan.

The Transjordan Tribes Pledge Aid (1:12-18)

Now Joshua speaks particularly to three groups: the Reubenites, the Gadites, and the half-tribe of Manasseh. He specifically reminds them of Moses' command to join the other tribes in conquering Canaan. He does this because, as we know looking back, these tribes settled on the east bank of the Jordan. They already had, or were near, their land. It would be tempting for them to just settle down and let the rest of Israel take care of itself. The fact that these tribes' families remained on the east bank suggests that perhaps they already were rather established. Yet at God's command they joined the others in conquering the land to the west. From the conquest to the writer's own time, staying together has been essential for Israel's survival.

The tribe of Manasseh eventually settled partly on the east and partly on the west of the Jordan. Joshua here

JOSHUA, JUDGES, AND RUTH

addresses the eastern part of the tribe. The use of the term *half-tribe* shows that the writer was speaking from hindsight.

We must remember that the author had lived on the west side of the Jordan. To him, the land of Reuben, Gad, and Manasseh lay *beyond the Jordan*. To Joshua, at the time, their land would have been on *this side of the Jordan*.

Toward the sunrise means on the east.

The Spies (2:1-24)

Here is the story of one incident that helped make the conquest possible. In preparation for the invasion, Joshua sends two spies to Jericho so he may know just what Israel is up against. They enter the city and stop at the house of Rahab. She tells them that the Canaanites fear an Israelite invasion. Then she hides them and helps them escape. In return for her help and silence, the spies agree to protect her and her household when Israel attacks the city.

Shittim is the place where Israel is camped on the east bank of the Jordan. It lies across the river from Jericho.

Rahab was a *harlot,* or prostitute. Strictly speaking, the men should not have been associating with her. All the same, she was one who could be expected to know about prevailing attitudes and who might not be an especially loyal citizen. People might not notice the comings and goings of strangers in such a house. So Rahab was a fairly safe person for the spies to contact.

Conditions could be crowded inside a walled city. Archeology has uncovered many a house built right against the wall, using the city wall as part of the house. Thus, Rahab had a window on the outer wall. It proved a handy escape route for the spies.

§ § § § § § §

The Message of Joshua 1–2

In even this short passage we find many of the
Deuteronomists' basic ideas. We see a God active in
history, a God who commands and leads the people, a
God who is working to fulfill the promises made to
Israel. We see God offering help and strength from the
very onset of a difficult struggle. But God's help is
conditional; it depends on the people's faithfulness and
obedience to the law. The people's success also depends
upon their working together. The achievement of good is
a cooperative process. It requires cooperation of the
people with each other and with God. Only thus can a
strong, successful nation be formed and endure.

To us in our time this passage reiterates a timeless
biblical message. The almighty God cares for us, will
strengthen and guide us, and will fulfill the promises
made to us. We, however, bear a part of the
responsibility for our own success. We must obey God
and work cooperatively with others. God gives the law,
not simply to assert authority, but to guide us and to
keep us in fellowship with God. If we disobey, we will be
going against the grain of life, so we can only fall into
difficulty and failure. The tragic stories of many
individuals and nations who have made their own rules
attest to this wisdom from the ancient past.

§ § § § § § §

PART TWO

Joshua 3–5

Introduction to These Chapters

Now Israel is ready to take the big step. The people
will cross the Jordan and invade the land of Canaan. The
crossing itself is a miraculous one, a never-to-be-forgotten
event. God's power continues to work in this latest stage
of the people's struggle for freedom. God is still acting to
fulfill the promise.

These chapters, like the previous ones, contain traces of
many traditions. The author has skillfully joined them to
tell as completely as possible the story of one of the
greatest events in Israel's history.

Like all of Joshua, however, this is more than a story.
As striking as the events themselves is the attitude the
author conveys. At each step we see the people's
reverence, obedience, and worship. The author is very
concerned that we recognize the importance of these
attitudes. This is the work of a person who is trying to
preserve and enhance his own people's reverence and
faith.

We can see in these chapters some of the writer's other
concerns, too. We will note his interest in ritual, his
interest in preserving and magnifying liturgical forms, his
concern for remembrance of historical events and God's
actions in them, and his special interest in the law. The
writer wants us to know how Israel came into possession
of the land, but he also wants us to learn a religious
outlook on all of history. He wants us to see the power
and love of God at work in the lives of the chosen people.

Here is an outline of Chapters 3–5.

I. God Promises Help (3:1-13)
II. The Crossing (3:14–4:8)
III. The Crossing Completed (4:9–5:1)
IV. In Camp at Gilgal (5:2-15)

God Promises Help (3:1-13)

In these verses the people prepare to cross the Jordan. Joshua commands them to break camp and move forward. Then he outlines what will be happening. He explains that God is about to do a mighty act. This miracle will prove God's power and trustworthiness. Priests carrying the ark of the covenant will lead the people across the river. But it is the power of God that will make the difficult crossing possible.

We learn here that the Shittim camp is not on the river but slightly to the east. The people must move and set up camp again on the river bank.

In 1:11 Joshua said that in *three days* the people would cross the Jordan. The spies were gone *three days* (2:22). Now the people camp at the Jordan *three days*. Perhaps these are the same three days that the spies were gone, or perhaps we have here several stories, all of which are tied together with the idea of a three-day wait.

The *ark of the covenant* was the sacred box that held the Law. It represented God's powerful presence among the people. It also symbolized God's special covenant relationship with Israel and reminded the tribes of their mutual bond to each other within that covenant. Note the central place the ark takes in the miraculous crossing. The writer's special concern with the law puts it right in the forefront; it is an instrument of God's freeing power.

Two thousand cubits is about 1,000 yards. The need for such space shows the power of God. One must not get too close to sacred objects. The people must show reverence and awe in the presence of the almighty God.

Joshua's brief command to *sanctify yourselves* again shows the writer's interest in liturgical purity and his concern for that attitude of worship and reverence. This invasion is not just a military campaign; it is a highly significant religious experience. The people must prepare themselves spiritually and ritually for it.

Various ethnic groups living in Canaan at the time included Canaanites, Hittites, Hivites, Perizzites, Girgashites, Amorites, and Jebusites.

The phrase LORD *of all the earth* provides yet another emphasis upon God's power. It is an invitation to awe and reverence.

The Crossing (3:14–4:8)

The actual crossing of the Jordan parallels the crossing of the Red Sea. The deep waters of the Jordan are held back by God's power. The people can cross over on dry land. There are two striking differences, however. One is that now the enemy is before Israel, not behind. The other is that priests and the ark now play major parts in the event. Again, the writer's concern with ritual and law comes through.

It is April, the time when melting snow from the mountains floods the Jordan. The crossing would be especially difficult at this time. Therefore, the miracle of God's holding back the water is all the greater. One "natural" cause for the river's damming has been known to occur. That is a mild earthquake, which is not uncommon in the area. Such a quake could send debris into the river, diverting or stopping the flow for a time.

Adam is Adamah, a town upriver on the Jordan.

Zarethan is a city about twelve miles north of Adamah. It would not be exactly beside Adamah. There are some translation problems here, but the point seems to be that the water was dammed for some distance up the river.

The *salt sea* is the Dead Sea.

A representative of each tribe participates in the event

and in its memorial (*twelve men*). Again we see the emphasis upon unity—all the tribes have a part. The men are to take *twelve stones* to their next campsite. This is an act of reverence and a historical reminder. Thus the writer reinforces the importance of this miraculous event and the necessity of remembering God's act here at the Jordan.

The Crossing Completed (4:9–5:1)

The last of the people cross the Jordan River, the priests come out of the water with the ark, and the waters return to normal. The leaders of Canaan, hearing of the miracle, quake in fear because they know that God is with Israel.

The material contains a mixture of traditions. The message of God's power, however, comes through. At each step God commands, and Joshua obeys. God has made a great miracle. Not only Israel, but pagan peoples must recognize God's overwhelming might.

In verse 11 we note that the *priests leave the river*. In verse 17 Joshua commands the priests to come up out of the river. Here is another example of two traditions that have been brought together. The story is basically the same, but small details differ or are repeated.

In verse 9 Joshua sets up twelve stones in the Jordan. In verse 20 twelve stones are taken out of the Jordan. Perhaps Joshua prepared two memorials of the crossing. More likely, however, these are two different traditions. The point of each is the same: to recognize God's greatness and to remember it. *What do these stones mean?* Again the writer pounds away at the theme of remembrance.

The exact location of Gilgal is debated. However, it was certainly quite close to Jericho. *Gilgal* means *circle*. Perhaps a circle of twelve ceremonial stones gave it its name. The Israelites camped at Gilgal and used it as a major base for their invasion.

In Camp at Gilgal (5:2-15)

The people camp at Gilgal. The writer's concern for ritual purity appears strongly in these verses. All must be spiritually right before the conquest can begin. So the people observe two very important Jewish rituals, circumcision and Passover. Both rituals serve to bind together the disparate tribes, and both offer worship and obedience to God.

Circumcision is cutting the foreskin from the male genital organ. Other groups practiced circumcision, but in Israel it carried special significance. Circumcision was a sign of membership in God's chosen people. It was also a sign of obedience, a purification rite, and a symbol of God's covenant with the people. (See Genesis 17:9-14.)

The writer has difficulty explaining why the men are being circumcised. In verse 2 this is a *second circumcision*, but in verses 4-7 he explains that actually none of the boys born in the wilderness had been circumcised. Again, there were probably two traditions to explain a strong memory of circumcision rites at Gilgal. One other explanation exists: that some groups had not gone down into Egypt. When they joined the others, all who were uncircumcised were thus initiated, so that the common bond might be maintained and reinforced.

The name *Gilgal* is related to the Hebrew word *roll*. The writer uses the name of the place to emphasize the purifying aspects of the circumcision rite. God rolls away sin.

Passover celebrates the Exodus from Egypt, so it fits in quite well with the second crossing of a great water. The feast uses the last of the *manna*, the miraculous food God provided in the wilderness. On the next day unleavened cakes can be made of grain from the Promised Land itself.

When Joshua encounters God's representative, he must do just as Moses did at the burning bush: He must take off his shoes as a sign that this is an experience with the holy.

§ § § § § § §

The Message of Joshua 3–5

The message of the crossing is simple enough: God has unlimited power. God cares for the people, and will help them if they will remain obedient and reverent. Ritual is an important element of that obedience and reverence. Historical memories are also important because they remind us of God's great acts in the past and inspire awe, trust, and reverence in the present. Both remembrance and ritual help bind us to our fellow believers.

We today sometimes forget the vital role ritual can play in keeping us aware of God's greatness and trustworthiness. Certainly, ritual can be empty show. But if it is entered into with the heart, ritual can strengthen our faith. It can bind us in more trusting, more obedient fellowship with the almighty, loving God and with God's children.

§ § § § § § §

PART THREE Joshua 6–8

Introduction to These Chapters

Now the conquest begins. These chapters chronicle the first two battles, those at Jericho and Ai. The well-known battle of Jericho was a tremendous success. The battle at Ai was a very different story—a story of sin and discovery, and a story of defeat and eventual victory.

The material in these chapters comes from several different sources, some of them probably quite ancient. We find here many double versions of events. Sometimes these versions do not agree in every detail. Some stories may have become blurred or confused by age, yet they carry important memories of God's action in a crucial era of Israel's life. These the author has woven into a powerful narrative of both history and faith.

The author's main points remain as in previous passages: God's almighty power and the importance of obedience.

Here is an outline of Chapters 6–8.
 I. Preparations (6:1-7)
 II. The Fall of Jericho (6:8-21)
 III. Rahab Spared (6:22-27)
 IV. First Attack on Ai Fails (7:1-26)
 V. Victory at Ai (8:1-35)

Preparations (6:1-7)
God commands the people to march around Jericho on seven consecutive days. What a strange way to attack a city! Yet Joshua obeys in every detail. The priests and the

ark take their central place in the procession. On the
seventh day, to horns and shouts, the city will fall.

The liturgical symbols of priests and ark continue to
represent the presence of God's power. The writer's
interest in worship and ritual keep these factors at the
center of action throughout the conquest.

The passage speaks of seven days, seven priests, seven
trumpets, and seven trips on the seventh day. The
emphasis on seven probably comes from the writer's
concern for the sabbath (seventh). It is another detail that
shows the importance of religious tradition.

The ram's horn is another liturgical symbol. It is used
in Jewish worship to this day.

Encircling the city could be a way of laying claim to
territory. By tracing its borders the people stated that
they claimed all that was inside the circle.

The Fall of Jericho (6:8-21)

Joshua commands and the people do as God has
bidden. On the seventh day the horns blow, the people
shout, and the walls of Jericho fall. God's power is
obviously the cause. The people's obedience has been
rewarded. Now God commands that the city be utterly
destroyed. Only Rahab and her family are saved.

Archeology has shown that Jericho's walls did fall and
that the city was burned. However, the date of that
destruction does not coincide with the general era of the
conquest. Possibly an earlier victory by tribes related to
Israel has been incorporated here. That would still, after
all, be part of the history of Israel's occupation of
Canaan.

Notice that the text does not say that the shouts caused
the walls to fall. The people shouted, the horns blew,
and the walls fell. It is God's power that has destroyed
the fortifications—God's power abetted by the people's
detailed obedience.

There are at least two theories about just why the walls

fell. One is that the walls were weak, possibly left unrepaired by a sickly population. Another is that an earthquake might have occurred—the Jordan Valley does run along an unstable fault line. But this is not the author's way of thinking. He is trying to show the unparalleled power of God, not give a scientific explanation of each event.

The *trumpets* are ram's horns, not metal trumpets as we know them.

The reference to *shouting* is another instance of minor story variation. In 6:5 the horn is the signal to shout. In 6:16 the people wait for Joshua's command. In 6:20 there is confusion as to whether shouting or trumpets come first. Obviously this does not change the story's meaning at all. It simply shows that the writer probably had more than one version of the story to work with.

The ban, or *herem*, is total destruction. The people may take nothing as booty. The city will not be occupied. Everything in it must be destroyed except the precious metals, which must go into the Lord's treasury. This practice incorporates several ideas. One is the complete annihilation of God's foes. No ungodly person or thing should be left to taint Israel. Another is that the victory is presented as a sacrifice to God. The people get no material reward. They recognize that the victory is God's alone. They are risking battle in obedience to God, not for the gain of booty.

Or perhaps the city was afflicted with disease. Snails which serve as intermediate hosts for a parasite that causes schistosomiasis have been found in Jericho. Second Kings 2:19 states that the water in Jericho is bad. This might explain the total destruction, but it does not explain why Rahab and the metal objects were spared. Certainly the author sees the destruction as primarily an act of reverence and obedience. The people must prove their absolute loyalty by resisting the temptation to take articles of value that rightly belong to God. After all, it was God's power that brought the city down.

The writer shows no concern for the people of Jericho.
Possibly he has not gone so far as to consider God's love
for everyone. Or perhaps he is so intent upon illustrating
God's absolute power and the need for absolute
obedience that he cannot deal with such a complicated
issue.

Rahab Spared (6:22-27)

Joshua keeps faith with the spies' promise to Rahab.
Her cooperation with God is rewarded. The city's
destruction then proceeds as commanded. The prostitute
who hid Joshua's spies now joins the people of Israel.
Eventually she will wed Salmon, bear a son, Boaz, and
through him become an ancestress of David and of Jesus.

The curse on Jericho is a solemn, permanent thing.
Jericho is off limits forever. In 1 Kings 16:34 Hiel of Bethel
attempts to rebuild Jericho and reaps the tragedy of the
curse.

First Attack on Ai Fails (7:1-26)

Joshua moves on to Ai. He sends out spies, but they
are overconfident. The city is on a high ridge and is
stronger than the spies suspected. Joshua, believing that
God is with him, cannot understand the defeat. Then he
learns that there is another reason for that defeat.
Someone has sinned by secretly taking booty from
Jericho. The man, Achan, is found. He and his family are
stoned and burned. The importance of obedience becomes
painfully obvious. Another idea also appears, that the act
of one member can taint the entire group. Israel is an
entity, not a collection of individuals.

Ai means *the ruin*. It is about eleven miles north of
Jerusalem. Archeology has shown that it was a ruin even
in Joshua's time. Possibly the story has been confused
with the conquest of nearby Bethel, or perhaps an ancient
conquest story has attached itself to Joshua's feats. In any

case, the writer's point that sin breaks the people's relationship with God stands out clearly.

The name *Achan* is related to the Hebrew word for *trouble*.

Tearing the clothes (*rent their clothes*) and putting dirt on the head were signs of grief.

Joshua's anguished attempt to understand his defeat echoes Israel's cries in the wilderness. There they began to lose heart and accused Moses of leading them out of Egypt only to die in the desert (see Exodus 16:3).

A God who allowed the people to suffer defeat would be considered powerless. Joshua wants God to vindicate *thy great name* (verse 9) and show God's power.

Sanctify the people again points up the concern for ritual purity.

The text does not say so, but it appears that Achan was discovered by using the sacred lots. He took a mantle of Shinar (a cloak from Babylon or made in Babylonian style), about 5.9 pounds of silver, and 1.25 pounds of gold.

The *Valley of Achor* is the Valley of Devastation. This is where the people took Achan to kill him. It is quite a distance from Ai and may be connected to Achan because both the place and the man's name are related to the word *trouble*.

The *heap of stones* served as a burial mound, but was also a permanent reminder of the consequences of disobedience. The author returns to his theme of remembering the lessons of history.

Victory at Ai (8:1-35)

Achan's sin has been punished. The relationship between God and Israel has been restored. Now the conquest of Ai can go forward. God promises victory. Joshua obtains that victory by a very clever strategy. He sets up an ambush behind the city. With his main force he draws the Ai soldiers out. He feigns retreat, the hidden force sets fire to the city, then both groups attack the confused enemy. This time God allows Israel to take *spoil and booty* from the doomed city.

Thirty thousand men is quite a large group for an ambush. Quite possibly this is a copyist's error for 3,000 or even thirty.

Verses 3-9 and 10-12 are parallel accounts of Joshua's preparations.

Mount Ebal is a mountain to the north near Shechem. It stands opposite Mount Gerizim. The two form the sides of an important east-west pass. Mount Ebal is quite a distance from Ai, so this story may not belong here in the history. Still, it serves the writer's purpose: to show Joshua's obedience in offering worship and thanks to God as Moses had commanded. As usual, the writer emphasizes the place of the law in the Mount Ebal ceremony. His concern with ritual and liturgical correctness shows also in the care he takes to mention *peace offerings and burnt offerings,* two specific kinds of sacrifices. Similarly, the writer gives particular details of the altar construction.

Some persons not originally born into Joshua's group (*sojourners*) are here incorporated and given full membership privileges.

God must be obeyed and revered completely. No omissions or exceptions should be made, especially where the law is concerned. Therefore there was *not a word which . . . Joshua did not read* (verse 35).

§ § § § § § §

The Message of Joshua 6–8

Obedience—total, complete obedience—that is the key.
Achan's disobedience ruined Israel's attack on Ai.
Correction of this sinful situation made success possible.
The writer never wavers from this basic point: When
Israel is obedient, God will bring success. If Israel
disobeys, failure will ensue.

We may offer some objections to the writer's simple
formula. Life is sometimes more complicated than the
writer would make it appear. Still the kernel of truth is
there. Sin breaks people's relationship with God. They
then have no access to this strength when they need it.
There is no substitute for living as God has told us to
live.

§ § § § § § §

PART FOUR Joshua 9–12

Introduction to These Chapters

After spectacular successes at Jericho and Ai, Joshua moves on to conquer the rest of God's promised land. Chapters 9 through 12 tell the story of that conquest.

Joshua now faces a more complicated situation. It is no longer a matter of fighting one city at a time. Word of Israel's military feats has spread. Canaanite leaders recognize the grave threat facing them. So, they begin to join together for defense. One group coalesces in the south and one in the north. Joshua will have to deal with both these larger coalitions. In addition one city, acting independently, tries a different strategy, a combination of treachery and diplomacy. This complicates matters slightly, but God helps Joshua through it all to eventual victory.

In these four chapters the writer paints a rather majestic picture of Israel sweeping over Canaan by God's great power. The story is told quickly. The victories are complete. A brief note in Chapter 11, however, states that the war took a long time. Naturally, it would. Yet the writer has chosen to compress the action so he can bring out his point, the mighty and irresistible power of God which has given Israel the land of promise.

As in previous chapters, the writer has used several sources. Many of these may be very old and carry excellent historical memories. Some may have become confused over time. This much we know: Israel did overcome the Canaanites and did settle in Palestine, there to remain until 587 B.C.

Here is an outline of Joshua 9–12.

Treaty With the Gibeonites (9:1-27)

Joshua has just completed two impressive victories. The Canaanites are becoming alarmed. Some cities are already joining together for mutual defense. One city, however, decides on a different approach. From Gibeon, a group of men set out in ragged clothes, worn-out shoes, and carrying stale food. They come to Joshua in his camp at Gilgal, claiming to be ambassadors from a distant country. The worn shoes and stale food serve as "proof" of the distance they have traveled. They ask for a treaty. Joshua is at first suspicious. His mission is to wipe out the inhabitants of Canaan. What if these men are really Canaanites? Joshua could be going against God's orders. But a treaty with a country far away would not be wrong. Finally he is convinced. He makes the treaty. Then, only three days later, he discovers the trick. Now he is caught between God's original command and the oath he swore by God's name to the Gibeonites. The solution: Do not kill the Gibeonites, but make them slaves. Thus the writer explains the continued presence of Gibeonite slaves in Israelite society.

Here a *king* is the ruler of a single city.

Canaanites on the west side of the Jordan, *kings beyond the Jordan*, were beginning to form coalitions against Joshua. The territory mentioned covers most of Palestine.

Gibeon was a city six miles northwest of Jerusalem. It was a strong city that had been in league with three other nearby towns.

Hivites were a non-Israelite group living in central Palestine. We know little about the Hivites. In the Old

Testament the name is sometimes confused with *Horites,*
and sometimes the Hivites of Gibeon are called *Amorites.*
So, we cannot be sure just what ethnic group these
people belong to.

Verse 14 notes that the Israelites *did not ask direction;*
they failed to ask God's guidance before deciding upon
the treaty. Thus they fell into the Gibeonite trap.

The Gibeonites eventually became temple slaves. Verse
23 reflects that later situation for, of course, no temple or
house of worship had yet been built. The remark, *the
house of my God* reflects, too, the writer's interest in
religious places and activities. The story of Gibeonite
treachery helps explain why non-Israelites serve in God's
house.

Southern Campaigns (10:1-43)

Gibeon was a strong city. The southern kings had
apparently counted on Gibeon to help in their fight
against Joshua. Instead, Gibeon made peace. Now the
southern kings are both frightened and angry. They
decide to attack Gibeon, perhaps hoping to force the
Gibeonites to join them. But the Gibeonites appeal to
Joshua for protection. So Joshua is in the difficult position
of having to defend one Canaanite group against another.
No matter. He would have had to fight the southern
coalition sooner or later anyway.

Despite the mess Joshua has gotten into, God still
promises to be with him. Through the night Joshua
marches his men the twenty miles to Gibeon. There he
takes the southern kings with a surprise dawn raid. The
Canaanite forces panic and retreat. As they run, God
sends hailstones upon them. Sun and moon even join to
aid Joshua. The kings attempt to hide in a cave, but they
are found and slaughtered. Joshua then moves through
their cities, removing any remaining resistance. Finally he
returns to camp at Gilgal.

Jerusalem, Hebron, Jarmuth, Lachish, and Eglon are cities of the south. (See map, page 155.) Eglon is also a personal name. There is some question about whether Eglon is here a city or the king of a city (Debir). In Joshua 12:12-13 both Eglon and Debir are listed as cities.

The writer makes a point to note that more men died from God's *hailstones* than from the warriors' blows. He wants to make sure that we realize this is God's victory.

There has been much debate over the event in verse 13, *the sun stood still.* Some have suggested that the poem should read, *Sun, cease from shining*—be dark or cloudy so Joshua might sneak up on his foes more easily or so that his soldiers will not wilt in the heat. This is not generally accepted, however. Meteor showers and an eclipse have also been suggested as the event behind the poem. But these ideas are not too satisfactory either. Best is a recognition that this is a poem, a work that uses symbols to powerful effect. At the time many people worshiped the sun and moon as deities. The poem shows that Israel's God has power far beyond any pagan imaginings. The sun and moon are God's, to use as God wishes. And Israel's victory is God's wish.

The *Book of Jashar* is a collection of ancient songs.

Makkedah is the site of the cave where the kings tried to hide. The location is uncertain, but it was apparently in the area of Gibeon.

Five trees and *great stones* are landmarks that help make the story more vivid and more memorable.

Putting *feet upon the neck* of a conquered enemy is a common sign of victory.

We have just learned that Joshua defeated the five kings and their armies. Now we learn that the cities and their kings must be conquered individually (verses 29-43). This Joshua does with dispatch. It is possible that the survivors needed to be eliminated and that new kings had risen in the cities. However, it is more likely that this is simply a different version of the earlier story.

Notice that the writer does not list Jerusalem as a city

that Joshua conquered. He knows that Israel never occupied Jerusalem until David took it.

He left nothing remaining is a phrase repeated throughout to emphasize Joshua's complete obedience to God.

Northern Campaigns (11:1-23)

Kings from northern Palestine have also joined to fend off Israel's advance. Some of this area is a plain. Kings from these cities have chariots and horses, weapons which Israel does not have. Still, God promises victory. An important part of the strategy will be to hamstring the horses and burn the chariots.

Joshua does as he has been told. In a surprise attack he cripples the horses before they can be hitched up, sets fire to the chariots, and routs the assembled army. Then he turns back to overcome their individual cities. This time the Israelites are allowed to take booty, but they must kill all the inhabitants.

Hazor, Madon, Shimron, Achshaph, Naphothdor, and *Mizpah* are cities or territories in the north. (See map, page 155.)

Hazor's king headed the northern confederation, and his is the only city in this area that was burned.

Arabah sometimes refers to the Dead Sea. Here, however, it includes the whole Jordan valley.

Chinneroth is the Sea of Galilee.

Meron is probably a creek flowing from the mountains of upper Galilee to the Sea of Galilee.

The writer is emphatic about the total destruction of Israel's foes, saying that there were *none left that breathed* (verse 11).

Although the writer makes the conquest seem swift, the author of this portion recognizes that the fight for Canaan was a difficult one, and took *a long time* (verse 18).

If the Canaanites had given up without a fight, there would have been no need to slaughter them. Yet the writer knows from later history that Canaanite elements remaining within Israel made it easy for the people to turn toward idols. He believes that God does not want Canaanites mixed in with the chosen people. So, he says that God *hardened their hearts* against Israel. Thus, there is an excuse for their total destruction. This may seem odd thinking to us, but the writer has a message to convey about the importance of staying clear of pagan influences, and this is one way he does it.

The *Anakim* are a race of giants. In verse 22, the writer recognizes that some of this group remained in cities on the coast. One of those cities, Gath, later gave the world Goliath.

Conclusion (12:1-24)

This is a summary of Joshua's conquest. It differs at some points from the previous accounts. Possibly this portion comes from a separate source. The chapter includes information about conquests on the west side of the Jordan as well as those on the east. In verses 12 and 13 Eglon and Debir appear as two cities, whereas the earlier accounts listed Debir as king of Eglon.

§ § § § § § §

The Message of Joshua 9–12

Power and gift—if one had to characterize the message of Joshua 9–12 in a few words, these two would do it well. The stories of swift, total conquest show God's tremendous power working at every turn. The miracles, the sudden victorious attacks, the enemies' panic emphasize God's unlimited force. Gift, while it never appears in the text, is a central point of the stories. The Promised Land has been conquered, not by Joshua's brilliance nor by Israel's strength, but by the power of God. Israel has not earned the land; it is a gift from God. So the meaning is this: The almighty God cares for the people, fights for them, and will give them the gifts that have been promised to them. For their part, they must remember that what they have is not theirs by merit, but as a gift from God. That core message is as valid for us today as it was 2,500 or more years ago.

§ § § § § § §

Joshua 13–21

Introduction to These Chapters

The main battles are over. Joshua and his people have general control of the Promised Land. Now it is time to settle down. Chapters 13–21 tell how the twelve tribes, by lot, obtained their portions. The author gives detailed listings of cities and boundaries assigned. Chapters 20 and 21 also detail the establishment of two special kinds of cities. In the land distribution, as in the battles before, *God* is the commander and supervisor.

The material in these chapters comes from many sources. It is even more of a jumble in spots than we have found in previous chapters. The lists of towns and boundaries come from various times and appear to have been updated here and there along the way. So, we cannot be sure exactly what lands the tribes received at the actual time of conquest. The lists do give us a general idea, however. The map on page 155 shows the approximate area each tribe occupied.

One question has bothered scholars: Did the tribes really distribute the land by lot as described, or do the lists merely reflect geographical realities—the places where each tribe eventually chose to settle? The boundaries as given probably do reflect some natural settlement patterns and population shifts over the centuries. The fact, however, that the text gives us two accounts of a distribution at two different sites, suggests that some sort of initial planned distribution did take place under the leadership of Joshua.

These chapters include another small problem, that of the twelve tribes. Here and in many other Old Testament books the number twelve is highly significant. Yet we can find differing lists of tribal names. The twelve tribes that receive territories here are: Reuben, Gad, Judah, Benjamin, Simeon, Asher, Dan, Zebulun, Issachar, Naphtali, Manasseh, and Ephraim. But Levi and Joseph were two of Jacob's twelve sons. What about them?

The tribe of Levi is called by God to serve as priests. They have no specific territory but are assigned certain cities throughout Israel. Joseph also receives no allotment. However, two of Joseph's sons, Manasseh and Ephraim, receive shares. The total of territories thus remains at twelve.

These chapters show God's people working together at God's command to form a cohesive nation. The author, writing in exile, was especially concerned with the tribes sticking together. His attention to the details of ancient land holdings, as those details had come down to him, may also reflect his exilic setting. After all, if the people were soon to return home, it might be important to remind everyone just who was supposed to own what. It would also help to maintain hope if people could remember that God had given them this land. The boundaries the writer describes are, of course, ideal ones. Israel very seldom controlled territory that actually matched this description.

These chapters may be outlined as follows.
 I. Land Still Unconquered (13:1-7)
 II. Inheritance of the Transjordan Tribes (13:8-33)
 III. Division Among Remaining Tribes (14:1–19:51)
 IV. Special Cities and Conclusion (20:1–21:45)

Land Still Unconquered (13:1-7)
Joshua's sweep of Palestine is over. Israel controls most of the land. Yet some areas remain unconquered. We

know from later history that some of this territory would never be taken, or would be held only briefly. Most of this unconquered land lies in the west near the Mediterranean and in the hills to the north. In Judges, Samuel, Kings, and other books we will find numerous military struggles in these areas. For now, though, God commands that the people distribute and take hold of the land. God promises to drive out before them any remaining foes.

Joshua will be distributing land on the west side of the Jordan to *nine and one-half tribes*—nine tribes plus half of Manasseh. We noted in Chapter 1 that two and one-half tribes had already been promised land on the east side of the river.

Inheritance of the Transjordan Tribes (13:8-33)

Here we read of the land east of Jordan that belonged to Reuben, Gad, and half of Manasseh. The text indicates that Moses had already set these tribes' inheritance. You can see approximately where these tribes settled in the map on page 155.

The east bank tribes failed to drive out the Geshurites and the Maacathites (verse 13). This note may be simply an explanation of these Canaanites' presence within Israel. It may, however, also be a mild rebuke for Israel's not completing the task of clearing out the land.

The tribe of *Levi* is one of priests and religious teachers. Levites served in sanctuaries and later in the Temple, but ranked lower than the priests descended from Aaron. Levitical priests cared for the sanctuary and its equipment, served as musicians, taught and interpreted the law, and helped in the administration of justice. The Levites received no exclusive territory. Instead they were assigned to key cities throughout Israel.

Division Among Remaining Tribes (14:1–19:51)

Here the writer describes the distribution of the land to

the west of the Jordan. In Chapter 14 the distribution takes place at Gilgal; in Chapter 18 it takes place at Shiloh. The two locations suggest that the writer had two versions of the story available to him.

The map on page 155 shows the approximate areas each tribe received. As we mentioned earlier, these ancient boundary lists may have been altered over time. As they stand now, the boundaries recorded in Joshua correspond fairly well with land areas held in the time of David.

Land allotted to three individuals receives special note. The men are Joshua, Caleb, and Othniel. Joshua, having led the people faithfully, receives a city of his choice in the Ephraimite hills. Caleb, Moses' other confident spy, receives the city he spied upon, Hebron. The special attention given to Othniel is a little more complicated. He has taken a city and received Caleb's daughter for his wife as a reward. His land allotment, however, is arid. His wife, therefore, asks her father to provide access to water for them. This Caleb does. The story is important because it explains why a particular group in the Negeb has claim to certain springs.

Notice that, while earlier accounts suggested that Joshua had thoroughly conquered the land, here the tribes must still take their land from some remaining inhabitants. The Anakim, for instance, are still at Hebron. This is yet another instance of multiple traditions.

Before Israel entered the Promised Land, Caleb, along with Joshua and ten others, spied out the land. He was a Kenizzite, a member of a clan of Edom. He was not, therefore, an Israelite by blood. This bit of information seems meant to explain the membership of some foreign elements within Israel. The story of Caleb's inheritance appears twice, in 14:13 and in 15:13.

Othniel is a kinsman, not a full brother, to Joshua. They come from the clan of Kenaz but have different fathers.

The *Negeb* is a very dry area in the south of Palestine.

The tribe of Joseph has been divided into two parts, Ephraim and Manasseh. Half of the Manasseh tribe receives land on the west bank. In 16:9-10 Ephraim has some towns within Manasseh's territory.

Shiloh maintained an important sanctuary for many years. The ark of the covenant remained in Shiloh until it was taken by the Philistines in 1050 B.C.

The total of cities in 15:36 is fifteen, not fourteen.

The list in 19:6 includes fourteen, not thirteen cities.

The tribe of Dan (19:47) lost its original inheritance. It then moved to Leshem (Laish), and changed that city's name to Dan.

Special Cities and Conclusion (20:1–21:45)

God has already commanded that the people set up two special kinds of cities. These are the cities of refuge and the Levitical cities. These cities would play particular roles in establishing and maintaining Israel's national strength.

Cities of refuge were places where a person who had accidentally killed someone could go for safety until a trial could be held. Otherwise a lynch mob of the deceased's relatives would dispatch him immediately.

Levitical cities were the places where Levites would settle. There is some confusion in the Old Testament about whether or not Levites actually owned this land exclusively. Whatever the situation, these cities scattered throughout the land assured that religious workers would be spread across the area.

These two special kinds of cities aided Israel's development greatly, especially in its early years. The cities of refuge helped avoid needless infighting and ongoing vendettas. The Levitical cities made religious teaching and worship widely available. These cities made it easier for the tribes to stick together, to solidify their common family identity, to maintain a constant faith, and to continue sharing a common religious heritage.

Foreigners (*strangers*), as well as Israelites, could use the cities of refuge. This might easily eliminate some unnecessary foreign wars. It was also a mark of compassion, an important factor in Israel's ethical development.

Hebron is a city of refuge, a Levitical city, and the inheritance of Caleb. The writer tries to explain this complicated situation in 21:11-31 by saying that the fields outside the city were actually Caleb's.

There were forty-eight Levitical cities (21:41), approximately four to each tribe, although division was not exactly equal.

§ § § § § § §

The Message of Joshua 13–21

By following God's commands, Israel was able to establish an orderly, cohesive nation. Fair division of land, plus establishment of Levitical cities and cities of refuge, reduced the probability of internal quarrels. The tribes could live together in peace and, with that internal peace, would gain strength to face external foes. Most important, these institutions that would make the nation strong came from God. God, even now, was still providing for the people.

More generally, the message is that God does want the people to live in peace. God not only wants this, but works to help it happen. God provides institutions and processes that make it easier to get along together. Our part is to obey commands and to use the institutions and rules God has given to develop a good communal life.

§ § § § § § §

Joshua 22–24

Introduction to These Chapters

These chapters mark the end—the end of Israel's
conquest period, the end of Joshua's life, and the end of
the Book of Joshua. The largest battles are over. The
tribes from east of the Jordan can go home. The
remaining tribes can move to their assigned territories.
The people can work in peace to build a new nation. And
yet, misunderstanding of one event, the building of an
altar, threatens to undo everything. The matter is settled,
however, and the nation remains intact.

This is obviously a crucial point in Israel's history, a
time for reflection and stock-taking. We find these
attitudes in two farewell addresses given by Joshua. They
wrap up all that Israel's experience and Joshua's own
example have taught throughout the book. In the first
address Joshua pleads with the people to obey God so
they may continue to prosper in God's strength. In the
second he leads the people in a covenant renewal, a
conscious pledge to continue serving God alone. This end
is a new beginning, the start of a new phase of
nationhood. It is a phase to be lived, like past phases, in
faithful obedience.

This section, like the rest of Joshua, has been pieced
together from several sources. Some are probably ancient
remembrances handed down over the centuries. What the
various writers have done with these remembrances
reflects the special concerns of the periods in which those
writers lived. One important period was the time of King

Josiah (640–609 B.C.). A second major period was the Exile (587–538 B.C.). Idolatry, intermingling with Canaanites, and ritual correctness were major concerns from Josiah's time on. The tragic consequences of faithlessness and God's geographically limitless presence were significant ideas during the Exile. Other themes, like national unity and Israel's covenant with God, were important in many periods.

The book climaxes with Joshua's dramatic challenge to covenant renewal at Shechem. This climax is an extremely effective way of placing before readers the book's central point: the importance of obedience and faithfulness.

Here is an outline of these chapters.

I. Departure of the Transjordan Tribes (22:1-34)
II. Farewell Address (23:1-16)
III. Covenant at Shechem (24:1-28)
IV. Three Burials (24:29-33)

Departure of the Transjordan Tribes (22:1-34)

The scene is Shiloh. The main conquest is over. Joshua blesses the tribes of Reuben, Gad, and half of Manasseh as they prepare to cross back over to their homes east of the Jordan. Joshua reminds them to obey the law and to serve God faithfully. Then he sends them off with their share of the collected spoils.

Their departure is not without problems, however. At the Jordan these tribes decide to build an altar. When the other tribes hear of this altar they are incensed. They send representatives to discipline the eastern tribes for what seems to them a terrible religious offense. It nearly comes to war until the eastern tribes explain that they had no intention of making sacrifices there. The altar is to be a memorial and a reminder to all concerned that the eastern tribes are part of Israel, partaking of the same religious beliefs and traditions. God lives on the east as well as on the west bank of the Jordan. This accepted, the tribes again separate in peace.

Why such a fuss over an altar? Early in Israel's history many altars and holy places stood throughout the land. But King Josiah outlawed these holy places. Idolatry had flourished there. Worship should thereafter be controlled by keeping it in Jerusalem. Joshua's people may have feared idolatry among the eastern tribes, but the person most concerned about this altar is really the later writer who had actually seen the proliferation of idolatry in outlying sanctuaries. The conflict and its resolution reflect many of the religious problems Israel had to solve over the centuries, including the questions of worship regulation and the limits or non-limits of God's presence.

Bashan is land east and to the north of the Jordan.

Gilead is another area east of the Jordan.

We do not know the exact spot where the altar was built. It seems, however, to have been on the west side of the Jordan River because one of its functions was to remind the western tribes that their brothers across the river still belonged to Israel. For the writer in exile, this altar incident might have served to remind people that God is God everywhere, not just in the territory of western Palestine.

Peor is a spot located in the Moab area where Israel became involved in idolatry before entering the land of Canaan. (See Numbers 25.) Note here, as in the story of Achan, that the sins of a few can contaminate the whole nation.

Phinehas is a priest who leads the deputation confronting the eastern tribes. He is the same one who helped settle the problem of idolatry of Peor.

Farewell Address (23:1-16)

This is the first of two addresses Joshua gives. The place is not mentioned. The speech itself is in two parts. Verses 3-10 concentrate on God's promise and its fulfillment. Verses 11-16 are a warning against the temptations of intermarriage and idolatry. Later writers knew all too well the awful consequences of Israel's yielding to such temptations. Joshua's speech is, in fact, a succinct statement of one of the book's basic points: God will be with you just as long as you remain faithful.

Covenant at Shechem (24:1-28)

Joshua's second address comes at Shechem. Here he recounts Israel's history from the call of Abraham through the Exodus to the conquest. He emphasizes that God's power has done all this. Then he challenges the people to put away all other gods. Joshua makes a resounding pledge for himself and his family. The people respond with a similar pledge. Then the tribes leave, each to its own inheritance.

The presence of two farewell addresses suggests two separate traditions, each showing Joshua's concern for Israel's future.

The northern city of Shechem stood between Mount Ebal and Mount Gerizim. It was the site of a long-standing and important shrine.

God sending a *hornet* into battle before Israel may refer to the use of insects as weapons. Since Egypt was sometimes represented as a hornet, the term could also suggest Egypt's weakening of Canaan some years before Israel's entrance. However, the most likely explanation is that the hornet is a symbol of God's great ferocity and power.

The River (verse 14) is the Euphrates. Abraham's family originated in Mesopotamia, where they were pagans.

Joshua warns Israel of possible weakness, saying, *You cannot serve the LORD*. Perhaps, too, he is using reverse psychology to make the people more determined to remain faithful.

The shrine at Shechem was built around a sacred oak tree.

Three Burials (24:29-33)

The book ends with the notice of three burials: Joshua's, Joseph's, and Eleazar's.

Joshua was buried at the town he had chosen, Timnathserah. A brief eulogy (verse 31) shows Joshua's influence. The writer notes that Israel served God all of Joshua's days and even after his death, so long as any of his contemporaries remained.

Joseph had died much earlier in Egypt. When the people left, they took Joseph's bones with them. They finally buried the bones in Joseph's family tomb at Shechem. (See Genesis 50:25-26.)

Eleazar was the son of Aaron and father of Phinehas (the man who had mediated the quarrel over the altar). Eleazar was buried in Phinehas's town of Gibeah.

§ § § § § § §

The Message of Joshua 22–24

These chapters, especially Joshua's speeches, pound away at a basic Deuteronomic point: God is the power that protects and saves you. If you remain faithful to God you will have success; if you do not, you will reap disaster. Joshua's challenge to the people at Shechem invites all to join in the congregation's affirmation: *we also will serve the* LORD, *for he is our God.*

The warnings about the temptations of idolatry are all too poignant. Israel had, by the time of the earliest Deuteronomic writers, forsaken God and gone after idols. Even when overt idolatry had been controlled, faithlessness continued. Finally, the nation had collapsed. Yet the call was still there. The people could still return to God. They could again affirm with Joshua: . . . *as for me and my house, we will serve the* LORD. The writer hoped that his people would do just that.

As for us, we have the glad and the sad experiences of Israel to learn from. We, too, are tempted to turn from God. But we, like Israel, can also respond to the challenge. We can choose this day, and every day, whom we will serve.

§ § § § § § §

Introduction to Judges

Name

The title refers to this book's main characters, the judges. The Hebrew concept of "judge" differs somewhat, however, from our American use of the word. The biblical persons called judges were tribal or national leaders. Often they were military commanders. Sometimes they settled disputes or offered advice. They gained their leadership positions informally or by popular acclaim. Many judges displayed exceptional wisdom, unusual skill in organization, or personal charisma. These were individuals in whom the people could see God's spirit at work. It was this divine spirit that gave the judges their talents. Since Israel had no king or other central political figure, the judges played an important role in Israel's survival. They provided administrative and military leadership to a new, loosely organized nation.

Classification

Jews consider this book the second of the "former prophets." And, like the Book of Joshua, it does exhibit a prophetic viewpoint. Christians, however, usually call this a historical book because it deals directly with the history of Israel and forms part of the epic historical work that includes most of Deuteronomy through 2 Kings.

Author

Who wrote the Book of Judges? That is a complicated question. Scholars believe that the book grew over several centuries. We can recognize at least four major steps in that growth. First came the oral tradition. From the actual time of the judges up to about 950 B.C. people told stories about these leaders, passing the tales on from generation to generation. Between 950 and 800 B.C. someone collected these stories and wrote them down. Around 615 B.C. one or more writers, whom we call the first Deuteronomic historians, included these stories in a great history of Israel. After the destruction of Jerusalem in 587 B.C., another historian of the Deuteronomic school edited a final version.

So, who was the author of this book? Many people were. But the persons who did the most to put the book in the form we have today were the Deuteronomic historians. These were the same ones who prepared and edited the final version of Joshua. For convenience we call them (or him) D. Where possible we also try to distinguish the time period a particular passage comes from.

Style

The style of Judges varies because so many people contributed to it. We find earthiness and a sense of humor mixed with judgmental comments and dry connecting paragraphs. Still, throughout the book we can see one obvious formula repeated over and over: *The children of Israel did evil in the sight of the Lord, and the Lord gave them into the hands of . . . and the children of Israel cried unto the Lord and the Lord raised up a deliverer . . . and the land had rest.* With this formula one of the later editors tied his string of stories together and made a theological point all at the same time.

Purpose

The writers' purpose was, of course, to preserve Israel's history. But it was more than that. D and the others wanted to convey the lessons of history, to show the nation what it must do to survive and prosper. These writers wanted to encourage faithfulness and obedience in a people who could easily go astray. They wanted to warn the people of the consequences of disobedience and to remind them that God could be depended upon, no matter what the danger.

The Times

What were the times like? Since the book grew over so many centuries we have to deal with several different times. First is the time of the judges themselves, 1200–1050 B.C. This was just after Joshua's conquest of Palestine and before Israel chose its first king. The time was a very unsettled one. Israel still had to fight to maintain its hold on the land. The nation was only loosely organized. It was surrounded by enemies, all trying to move into or regain land that Israel held. There was Ammon east of the Jordan, there was a Canaanite confederation in north-central Palestine, there were Philistines on the west, Moabites to the southeast, and Midianite nomads who ranged to the east and south of Israel. (See the map "The Ancient Near East," found on page 156.)

Israel was frequently at war with these enemies. Unity among the tribes was essential. But Israel had no king. God was to be their only ruler. So, in times of special need divinely inspired judges took on specific leadership tasks.

The religious situation under the judges was one of alternating faith and faithlessness. When they were faithful, the people depended upon God for protection and leadership. They recognized God's spirit working through the judges. The tribes periodically met to worship God at central sanctuaries, including Shiloh, Bethel, Gilgal, and Mizpah. Some individuals had home worship centers as well. Nonetheless, this was a primitive time. Faith and worship often went awry. Superstitution ran high, and divination was a common practice. Idolatry crept in. Ethics were not the highest. We find many cases of sexual laxity, treachery, thievery, and violence here. Low morality was common and was sometimes approved or taken for granted.

The time of the seventh-century historian was a more organized one. But Israel had fallen into gross idolatry. So, the seventh-century writer's concern focuses on pagan influence and idol worship.

By the time of the exilic editor, Israel's land had been destroyed. The defeated Jews feared that God had rejected them or was powerless to help them. This editor used the stories of the judges to show that an all-powerful God will continue to fight for Israel if the people will only respond in obedience.

Theological Perspective

The main theological points in Judges are the same as those of Joshua. The writer emphasizes God's power, desire to help Israel, and faithfulness in fulfilling promises, and the importance of obedience. If the people will obey, God will defend them and enable them to prosper. If they do not obey, disaster will befall.

Here, as in Joshua, we encounter a problem with violence. These stories frequently show God an advocate of bloodshed. Why would the biblical writers portray God this way? One reason lies in human nature. It is very easy in time of war to assume that God hates the enemy as much as we do. Ancient peoples were no different from ourselves in that respect. They gleefully reported every detail of the foe's defeat and attributed it all to a vengeful God. Second, we must consider that early Israel may not yet have come to recognize God's love for all people. Very old stories tend to think only of God's love for Israel. Third, a concern for preserving historical material or a reluctance to get into complex questions of God's character may have led a later, more sophisticated editor to let the ancient stories stand without revision or comment. A fourth possibility is that the writer saw God using the world as it is, not the world as we might wish it to be. In a violent world, God is shown moving in violent events toward long-term goals.

Conclusion

Judges, then, is not a simple book. It is an important one, though. It provides both vital historical information and a religious perspective on God's acts in history. This perspective is one that we need to consider in thinking through our own faith.

Judges 1

Introduction to This Chapter

After the death of Joshua . . .—with his first words the
writer links this book to the preceding one in his series.
We know that the history begun in Joshua is now
continuing in the Book of Judges.

Next we find a curious question: *Who shall go up first for
us against the Canaanites?* (verse 1). The Book of Joshua
has just told us all about Israel's conquest of Palestine.
Why now this question of who will go first to fight?
There are two possibilities. One is that this is a different
version of the basic conquest, one in which Joshua is not
a major hero. The second possibility is that after Joshua's
conquest the land was still not completely under Israel's
control. Joshua 14–18 suggests this kind of situation.
These stories, then, would be the stories of each tribe's
efforts to take control of its territory. Whatever the case,
we begin with a recognition that Israel had to fight for
the land. As the book goes on we realize that Israel must
continue to fight to maintain its possession.

Judges 1–2:5 is a complicated mixture of material. We
find here some duplicates from Joshua and some passages
that differ from the Joshua narrative. One big difference
is that now the tribes are working separately rather than
as a unit. Another is that there is no one leader. Only a
tribe, Judah, is mentioned as leading the way. We also
find some differences in the areas conquered. The battles
may have taken place after Joshua, or the differences may
be due to variations in ancient memories.

The purpose of this section is to preserve as much information as possible, to provide a transition from the Book of Joshua, and to establish this writer's unique interpretation of Israel's history in this period.

The outline of this section has just two parts:

I. Many a Battle (Judges 1:1-36)
II. Departure From Gilgal (Judges 2:1-5)

Many a Battle (Judges 1:1-36)

This section opens with the notice that Joshua has died. The writer then presents a series of battles which various tribes fight individually or in small groups. He repeats the story of Caleb's daughter, Achsah, and her request for a water source in her husband's arid territory. (See Joshua 15:16-19.) In verses 22-26 the writer tells a new story, the taking of Bethel. The Book of Joshua never mentions Bethel's capture. Now the tribe of Joseph gains access to the town with the help of a traitor.

Verses 27-36 show one of the writer's main concerns quite clearly. These verses repeatedly point out Israel's failure to drive out the Canaanite inhabitants. 1:19 showed Judah unable to drive out the inhabitants of the plain. In contrast, verses 27-36 do not say the tribes *could not*, but they *did not* drive out their enemies. This is a strong rebuke. The writer knew that these Canaanite remnants would eventually lead Israel into idolatry. Such faithlessness would one day bring disaster. So he points the finger, saying, "See, your history of disobedience stretches all the way back to your settlement in this land."

The people did try to follow God's will. They *inquired of the Lord*, probably by using the sacred lots, to determine which tribe should lead out.

Adonibezek was the prince of Bezek (location uncertain). Since Adonibezek eventually ended up in Jerusalem, it is possible that the name is a misspelling of Adonizedek, king of Jerusalem.

As Adonibezek's remark shows, mutilation (*cut off his thumbs and toes*, verse 6) was common practice. It not only humiliated the ruler, it made him unfit for battle.

Seventy kings (verse 7) is a large number. Seventy was also a standard size for a council. Adonibezek has taken, in his time, many important prisoners. Now he is reaping his due.

Captives usually ate table scraps (*pick up scraps*, verse 7).

Verse 8 speaks of an attack on Jerusalem. The attack was not totally successful, however. Verse 21 and Joshua 15:63 indicate that neither Benjamin nor Judah could evict the Jebusites from the city. Subsequent history indicates that Israel did not control Jerusalem until David took it.

Caleb was one of the spies who visited Hebron before Israel's entrance into Palestine. Of the twelve spies, only Caleb and Joshua believed that the land could be taken.

Othniel was a kinsman of Caleb. The term *brother* should not be taken literally. Both are from the non-Israelite clan of the Kenizites, but Caleb's father is Jephunneh (Joshua 15:13).

The *Negeb* is an arid area in the south of Palestine.

The *Kenites* were a people friendly to Israel who lived to the south of Palestine. Moses' father-in-law was a Kenite.

Jericho is sometimes called the *City of Palms*. The city here, however, is obviously another one far to the south.

Gaza is a city on the plain of southwest Palestine. Verse 19 belies the claim of victory in Gaza, indicating that Judah could not drive out its inhabitants. Over the years Israel seldom controlled this area effectively.

Chariots of iron (verse 19) indicates chariots with iron parts, not ones made completely of iron.

Land of the Hittites (verse 26) is the remains of an ancient empire in Asia and Syria.

The cities mentioned in verses 27-35 form two east-west chains of fortresses. These fortresses effectively hemmed in Ephraim and Manasseh on the north and south.

The *Amorites* (verses 34-36) are a Canaanite tribe.

Departure From Gilgal (Judges 2:1-5)

An angel now appears to offer Israel direct guidance. He moves Israel's base camp from Gilgal to Bochim. There he delivers a message from God, reminding Israel of God's act of deliverance in the Exodus. He speaks of God's promise to keep the covenant with Israel. Then he warns the people that failure to break away completely from the Canaanites and their religion will bring disaster. Again we recognize the writer's special concern. He knows that this is exactly what did happen.

Gilgal is a city near the Jordan in central Palestine. This was Joshua's main base throughout the conquest.

The location of Bochim is unknown. This city's name means *weepers*. In verse 4 the people weep at the thought of their possible disobedience. The move from Gilgal to Bochim may have poetic value: It parallels Israel's move from a position of obedience and victory to a position of disobedience and weeping.

§ § § § § § §

The Message of Judges 1

These verses are clearly a warning against the temptations of faithlessness and disobedience. The writer insists that God is faithful but that the people have not been faithful to God. They failed to complete the task of conquest God had assigned them. That failure would lead to idolatry and eventual ruin.

This is one variation of the message that the writer emphasizes throughout his history. Our success comes in obedience; our failure comes in disobedience. We today may recognize that all disaster is not necessarily the result of faithlessness. Yet, much of our misery, whether personal, national, or global, stems from someone's failure to live as God has intended. Perhaps we, like Israel, need to recognize the danger of our ways—and weep.

§ § § § § § §

Judges 2

Introduction to These Chapters

Another introduction—that's what we find in Judges 2:6–3:6. In the preceding section the writer had introduced us to the Book of Judges. He had made a clear transition from the Book of Joshua. He had told us of Joshua's death. Now here we find Joshua again. It looks like Judges 2:6–3:6 was the opening of an earlier version of the book. The final editor kept what he had and added an introduction of his own (1:1–2:5) before it.

The 2:6–3:6 introduction has two parts. Verses 6-10 form a connecting link to the Book of Joshua by reviewing Joshua's death and burial. The accounts of this hero's tribal dismissal and death echo Joshua 24:28-31. In 2:11–3:6 someone has written a summary of what we will find in the Book of Judges. It is a story of faithlessness and disaster, yet an affirmation of God's desire to save Israel if only the people will turn to God. This writer explains the role of the judges and how God used them to help Israel. The section concludes with two lists of non-Israelite peoples whose continued presence in Palestine contributed to Israel's downfall.

The material in these chapters obviously comes from several sources. We find numerous repetitions and variations. The writer apparently wanted to save every tradition, and did so despite the inconsistencies this created.

Within this material we find some important theological concepts. The writer outlines for us a pattern of events that will recur throughout the book. He sees the period of the judges as a repeating cycle of defection, oppression, prayer, and deliverance. Here and throughout the book he uses a set formula to begin a story: *And the people of Israel did what was evil in the sight of the* LORD (verse 11). The main point of the writer's whole historical epic comes through clearly in Judges: If the people obey God, they will prosper; if not, they will suffer. The writer (or several writers) also tries in these chapters to explain a theological puzzle, the problem of why God ever allowed these alien peoples to remain in the land when their presence caused so much trouble. In Joshua the answer was that Israel itself failed to rout the inhabitants. Israel thereby disobeyed God's command and suffered accordingly. In Judges 2:20-22 and 3:1-6 the writer provides additional explanations for the disastrous situation.

Here is an outline of this brief, but complex, section of Judges:

I. Joshua Dies (2:6-10)
II. Israel's Infidelity (2:11-23)
III. Israel Among the Nations (3:1-6)

Joshua Dies (2:6-10)

Joshua commands the tribes to go out from their common camp to settle in their allotted lands. Then Joshua dies, as does his whole generation. This passage is similar to, but does not have exactly the same wording as Joshua 24:28-31. Possibly that passage once ended the Book of Joshua while this one began the Book of Judges.

Judges 2:7 and 2:10 work together to set the scene for the rest of the book. The writer notes that the elders who had seen God's mighty works in the conquest remained faithful, but . . . *there arose another generation who did not know the* LORD (verse 10). That's what this book is about—the faithlessness of succeeding generations and

God's efforts to deal with them.

Timnathheres is a variant spelling of Timnathsereh. The *h* and *s* have been exchanged. Both spellings refer to the town Joshua inherited. Timnathsereh, used in the Book of Joshua, means *left-over portion*. Timnathheres, used here, means *portion of the sun*. The second version would be a little more flattering to Joshua, but it may be nothing more than a copying error.

Israel's Infidelity (2:11-23)

Verses 11-20 give us an outline for the book to follow. Over and over we will see the same sequence played out: The people forsake the Lord and go after Canaanite gods. God becomes angry and refuses to protect Israel. The people suffer. Then God pities them and gives them a leader or judge who saves them. Yet when the crisis has passed, the people again turn away.

In verses 20-22 the writer offers two reasons why God does not drive out all the Canaanites from the land. The first is that the people have already turned faithless. They have broken their covenant with God. God is no longer bound to protect them and, in anger, God refuses to remove the elements which are destined to bring Israel to ruin. The second explanation is that God wishes to test the people, perhaps setting up a kind of trial by fire which God hopes will strengthen and prove the people's loyalty. This second explanation makes God seem less of a punisher and more of a teacher.

In verse 23 we find ourselves back with Joshua again, remembering that God did not give Joshua complete victory over his foes.

One question might bear brief exploration here. That is, why should people to whom God has been so good turn so readily to Canaanite gods? There are several reasons. All of them together made idolatry an easy step for many Israelites.

The first is intermarriage. With so many Canaanites

around, such mixing was bound to take place. Once married, the Israelite could easily be drawn to the spouse's religion, if only to keep family peace.

Another reason for defection was familiarity. They saw the neighbors worshiping these gods, and they thought, why not? In addition, many Israelites may have remembered that their own ancestors worshiped just such idols as these.

A third temptation lay in the gods themselves. These were gods that offered what people desperately wanted: fertility of land and family, success in war, prosperity, and continued life. Such gods would be very attractive.

Not to be discounted, of course, is the nature of some Canaanite worship. These were fertility gods. They were worshiped by acts of sacred prostitution. Obviously this would be appealing.

So Israel did what was evil in the sight of the Lord *and served the Baals* (verse 11).

Baal is a Canaanite god. The term is usually plural because many worship centers, each with its own idol, flourished throughout Palestine.

Ashtaroth is the plural form of Astarte, the Canaanite fertility goddess.

In ancient Hebrew thought everything, good and evil, came directly from God. When God was angry God punished Israel by working against the people (. . . *hand of the* Lord *was against them for evil*, verse 15).

A *harlot* is a prostitute. This is a common religious metaphor. Israel has been unfaithful to God; she has played the harlot. The image is especially appropriate considering the nature of Canaanite religion.

Israel Among the Nations (3:1-6)

Here the writer attempts to list the peoples who remained within Israel and caused so much trouble. He has used at least two sources which do not agree. In verse 3 there are four nations: the Philistines, the

Canaanites, the Sidonians, and the Hivites. In verse 5 there are six groups: the Canaanites, the Hittites, the Amorites, the Perizzites, the Hivites, and the Jebusites.

Here again the writer tries to explain why God allowed these groups to remain. He offers two reasons: to test the people and to teach war. We have seen the testing explanation before, in verse 22. Teaching war may seem a little strange, but it can have two meanings: (1) to teach the people a painful lesson in obedience through the suffering of war, and (2) to let a new generation of people experience first-hand God's saving power in a major wartime crisis.

§ § § § § § §

The Message of Judges 2

This short passage carries several messages from several hands. The first and most prominent is the story of the later generations' infidelity and the suffering it caused. The second is God's effort to help. The third includes the explanations of why God allowed corrupting alien influences to remain within Israel: to punish, to test, to teach, or to bring the people back.

These verses speak of our frailty and of the weakness of second-hand religion. We, like the ancient Israelites, live among unbelievers. Our neighbors have values and practices that differ drastically from the biblical ideal. It is easy for us to accept their ways. It is easy to ignore God's commands. In the midst of these temptations, we need help. Unfortunately, it may take some suffering to make us realize that we need first-hand experience of God's power in our lives. That experience is one that we can only get through repentance and obedience.

§ § § § § § §

Introduction to This Chapter

Israel had established itself in Palestine. Still, the nations on every side continually pressed. Some wanted to recover territory Israel had wrested from them. All wanted to extend their holdings as far as they could. So Israel's claim to the land was often threatened. Power shifted from time to time and place to place. Sometimes Israel held its own; sometimes it didn't. The Deuteronomic writers set out to explain these changing fortunes from their own unique theological perspective. These events were not just political or military affairs; they were reflections of Israel's relationship with God.

With Judges 3:7-31 we begin the actual stories of the judges. These verses contain three ancient stories of men who saved Israel from encroaching enemies. None of the men is especially well-known today. Other biblical heroes have overshadowed them in the popular mind. This is due, at least in part, to the fact that these accounts are so short. The first is brief and tells only the basic facts plus their interpretation. The third is just one verse long. Only the second carries enough detail to really be a story.

The first and second stories follow the writer's characteristic formula. They begin, *And the people of Israel did what was evil in the sight of the Lord*. They worship idols. The Lord becomes angry and sells them into servitude. When the people cry to God for help, a deliverer is provided. The third story, being only a single verse, lacks the full formula. Yet, packed in among the others, it seems to follow the pattern.

Inclusion of these brief accounts shows the writer's determination to preserve all the historical material available. The repeated formula shows his concern to interpret the stories in theological terms.

The writer uses these and subsequent stories to show how Israel is supposed to relate to God. Here we begin a book-long series of examples where faithlessness breeds disaster while return to God brings salvation and peace. God is Israel's king and commander. Trust and obedience to this divine king is Israel's key to survival and success.

Here is an outline of these three accounts:

I. Othniel (3:7-11)
II. Ehud (3:12-30)
III. Shamgar (3:31)

Othniel (3:7-11)

In this first story the enemy who overcomes Israel is Cushanrishathaim. His center of power is not known. When the people cry to God for help, God sends Othniel as deliverer. This is the same Othniel who appears in Judges 1:12-15, the kinsman of Caleb who conquered Debir and married Caleb's daughter. Othniel is a Kenizite, that is, an Edomite. His clan has, however, been incorporated into the Israelite tribe of Judah. Of all the judges he is the only one from the south.

Verse 10 shows well the characteristics of a judge: the spirit of the Lord was upon him, he judged Israel, he went to war, and with God's help he overcame the enemy.

Cushanrishathaim means *double wickedness*. Verse 8 identifies him as king of Mesopotamia. The reference is rather vague. Possibly he ruled an area in northern Mesopotamia. Translation difficulties and historical factors make it hard to pinpoint his realm, however. Some commentators place Cushanrishathaim as a king of the southern hills. Wherever this conqueror came from, Othniel evicted him.

Ehud (3:12-30)

This is a much more detailed story than the other two in this section. Here we find many concrete facts and images. We can picture the events well—perhaps too well. This is a graphic presentation of an extremely gory event. The style, however, serves as indication of a very old story, told and retold, probably with some relish, by generations of rather primitive people.

The enemy now is Eglon, king of Moab. Moab is to the south. Eglon is, however, in league with the Ammonites and Amalekites. The Ammonites inhabit the central area east of the Jordan. The Amalekites are nomads who roam the territory generally. This confederation has moved westward into Jericho. The Israelites in the area must pay tribute. One might liken it to a combination tax and "protection" money.

Finally the people call to God, and God chooses Ehud to save them. Ehud is a characteristic early hero. He wins as much by treachery and wit as by strength. When he goes to deliver the tribute, Ehud carries a concealed sword or dagger. He hands over the money, then he and his company head toward home. Shortly, however, Ehud doubles back to Moab alone. He approaches Eglon claiming to have a special message for him from God. The message is Eglon's death. Ehud cleverly locks the door and escapes while the servants wait outside. Then Ehud marshalls troops from Ephraim and drives the surprised and kingless Moabite army back across the Jordan.

The *Amalekites* may have provided several of the Canaanite tribes with a kind of communications network. Moving around the territory as they did, they could carry messages from one tribe to another, making it easier for these enemies to gang up on Israel.

The *city of Palms* is Jericho.

Ehud was left-handed, probably because of a defect in his right hand. Ironically he was a Benjaminite, and Benjamin was the "son of the right hand." Left-handedness was considered quite unusual, but in Ehud's case it gave him a distinct advantage. Eglon would naturally be somewhat suspicious of even a lone visitor from Israel. He would be watching the right hand for signs of movement. When Ehud's left hand stirred, Eglon was caught off guard. Ehud killed him before he had a chance to defend himself. This is a good example of the Israelite underdog using a handicap to overcome a strong oppressor. Israel, being a small, weak nation, appreciated such stories immensely.

A *cubit* is about 18 inches.

Sculptured stones (verse 19) cannot be further identified. They may, however, be related to the stones Joshua took from the Jordan and set up in Gilgal (Joshua 4:20).

This story does not specifically say that God's spirit rested upon Ehud as upon the other judges. However, the idea of a *message from God* indicates that Ehud saw himself as God's agent.

Just what room the *rooftop chamber* may have been is not clear. The King James Version calls it a *porch*. It may have had two doors, one of which led to an outside balcony. If so, Ehud would have locked both doors and jumped to safety from the balcony. Or, Ehud may have locked a single door and escaped through a room inside the house while the servants were occupied elsewhere.

The location of *Seirah* is not known.

The quick marshalling of an army (. . . *and the people of Israel went down,* verse 27) shows Ehud's strong leadership qualities. The people saw him as God's deliverer and willingly followed him.

Shamgar (3:31)

This one verse is probably all the writer knew about Shamgar. The enemy now is the Philistines, who live to the west. The writer reports Shamgar as killing 600 Philistines single-handedly. Presumably this is an exaggeration, one which primitive people might enjoy very much. Whatever the actual facts, Shamgar was able to rid Israel of this Philistine menace.

Shamgar is probably a Hurrian name, suggesting that this hero may not have been a native Israelite at all.

Being the *son of Anath* may mean that Shamgar lived in Beth-Anath in Galilee (a Canaanite city) or that he was a member of a seminomadic tribe (the Hanaans) who sometimes provided mercenaries in the area. If Shamgar was a non-Israelite this would be one of many Old Testament examples of God's using foreigners to save the chosen people.

An *oxgoad* was a metal-tipped instrument used to prod oxen.

§ § § § § § §

The Message of Judges 3

This is a message of history. God has saved the people
many times. No matter how often they sin and suffer,
when they turn to God they will be saved. People of the
Exile knew suffering. The writer offers them the evidence
of history to show that there is hope. No matter what
Israel's sins (and they have been serious), God can still
raise up a deliverer.

The United States has not suffered invasion since its
early days. Still, our country could one day fall either from
external conquest or from internal weakness. The message
of Judges is that there is hope for a nation, even a nation
in deep trouble, if that nation will turn to the Lord.

For individuals, too, the message holds. No matter
what the sin or the suffering, God can help, if we will
only ask for help.

§ § § § § § §

Judges 4–5

Introduction to These Chapters

Content

These chapters tell the story of two judges, Deborah and Barak. Deborah is the leader and organizer; Barak is the military commander who carries out Israel's battle for freedom.

The place is Israel's northern territory. There enemies are confining Israel to the hills and denying access to the more prosperous plain areas.

The time is the twelfth century B.C., probably around 1125. Archeologists have discovered that Taanach, which figures prominently in the story, was destroyed about that time.

The enemy is a coalition of Canaanite kings or of Canaanites and Sea Peoples. These kings have strong armies with horses, iron chariots, and plenty of weapons. Israel is militarily weak and does not even know yet how to work with iron.

The problem, on the surface, is the oppression of these Canaanites. The people of Israel live in fear, shrinking back into the hills to avoid confrontation with the aggressive foe. Back roads are unsafe, caravans are unable to travel into Israel, farmers can scarcely work their land. But the underlying problem, as always in Judges, is Israel's faithlessness to God. Idolatry again has raised its ugly head, and Israel is suffering because of it.

The solution comes when the people finally call to God for help. God does respond by sending help, through Deborah and Barak. These two persons rouse the oppressed people to action. They call upon all the tribes of Israel to form an army. Some, but significantly not all, of the tribes respond. The day of battle comes. The weak, untrained tribesmen face their enemy. Then God, by storm and flood, destroys that enemy, giving Israel freedom and peace.

Structure

These chapters contain two versions of the same story. Chapter 4 is a prose account. Chapter 5 is a poem. That poem is one of the oldest pieces of Hebrew literature we have. It may well have been composed at the time of the event. The prose version of Chapter 4 may be a combination of two battle stories, one about a victory over Jabin and one about a victory over Sisera.

The two chapters tell essentially the same story, but they disagree on a few details. In Chapter 4 Jabin is king of Canaan, and Sisera is his general. Chapter 5 does not mention Jabin at all. Instead, we find the *kings* of Canaan, who are led by Sisera. Jabin appears in Joshua 11 as king of Hazor. His mention at this earlier time is one reason for suspecting that he does not quite fit into the Deborah story. His absence from Chapter 5 supports that suspicion.

A second difference in detail is the scene of battle. In Chapter 4 the battle is at the foot of Mount Tabor. In Chapter 5 the battle is at Taanach.

A third difference between the two accounts concerns who fought the battle. Chapter 4 mentions only the tribes of Zebulun and Naphtali. Chapter 5, however, gives these two special credit but indicates that other tribes also helped.

Despite these minor differences, each version makes the same point: God, through Deborah and Barak, saves Israel.

Purpose

The writer's general purpose in including these chapters was to preserve Israel's history and to inspire courage and faith, especially in times of oppression. The poem in Chapter 5, however, originally had some additional purposes. In the days before writing was common, it served as a teaching tool. It may also have served as a form of popular entertainment. But its most important function was probably to arouse enthusiasm and encourage action when Israelite armies again gathered to face a common enemy. This thrilling story of courage and victory would motivate the assembled recruits to bravery in the coming battle.

Style

Both these versions provide detailed, colorful accounts of events. Both are good examples of storytelling art, though perhaps the poem is a bit more dramatic. The writers build suspense, help listeners identify with Israel's cause and its heroes, and teach well their main points: the power and trustworthiness of God, the need for courage and faith, and the importance of cooperation.

A Moral Problem

In both these pieces, modern readers may find a common Old Testament problem. These stories reveal, even applaud, bloodthirstiness, vengefulness, and deceit. Jael is praised for her treachery and murder "in a good cause." Chapter 5 glories in the misery Sisera's mother experiences as she waits in vain for her son's return. These attitudes are foreign to us and must be recognized as such. Even God's chosen people did not fully understand God in those early days, nor perhaps do we yet.

Outline

Here is an outline of these chapters.

The Oppression (4:1-3)

As is usual in Judges, the writer begins with the formula *And the people of Israel again did what was evil in the sight of the LORD.* That evil brings oppression upon Israel. Finally they cry for help. The writer connects this story to the major story of Chapter 3 by noting that the former hero, Ehud, had died. Chapter 4 skips over Shamgar (Judges 3:31), but the version in Chapter 5 does mention him.

Jabin was a Canaanite king from Hazor, in the north. Joshua 11 tells us that Joshua killed Jabin before this story's opening.

Sisera was possibly one of the Sea Peoples. Chapter 5 shows him as a king in his own right, not as Jabin's general. His territory, Harosheth-ha-goiim, was probably near Megiddo, far from Hazor. Nevertheless, this somewhat confused account of the enemy may still indicate that Deborah and Barak faced some kind of confederation of Canaanites and Sea Peoples.

Deborah and Barak Plan (4:4-9)

Out of oppression the people have called. God has heard, and provides two leaders. The chief is Deborah, a prophetess. At God's direction she works with Barak to gather support from the tribes. They assemble an army. Barak insists that Deborah go with the army to battle. Barak knows that the spirit of God is with Deborah. For him, her presence assures the presence of God. Her presence would also make on-site divine guidance available. Deborah, in an almost teasing way, responds with an ironic prophecy. She tells Barak that he will not gain any great glory in this battle. The victory will come through a woman. First-time hearers of the story, and perhaps Deborah herself, would assume that Deborah is the woman. We learn later, of course, that the heroic woman is actually Jael. This is certainly excellent storytelling technique, but it may also be meant to suggest that a prophet like Deborah can speak with wisdom well beyond his or her own understanding.

Lappidoth is Deborah's husband. He is mentioned only here, so we know nothing about him except his name, which means *torch*.

Barak was apparently a leader from Kedesh. His name means *lightning*. Because of the similarity between "lightning" and "torch" some commentators suggest that Barak and Lappidoth may be the same man. This is possible, but with no more substantial evidence we cannot jump to such an identification.

The Palm of Deborah: Deborah had been acting as a judge, helping people solve problems and discerning God's will, for some time. She apparently had a wide reputation and had a special place where she could be contacted.

Kedesh was a town to the north near the Sea of Galilee.

The Victory (4:10-24)

The troops gather at Kedesh, then go to Mount Tabor. There they await the enemy. It is a strategic position for Israel: Sisera cannot go up into the hills with his chariots, but from the heights Israel can swoop down upon him. Deborah gives the battle cry. The Lord routs the enemy. The writer offers few details here, just the bare bones of events.

Sisera flees, leaving his troops to Barak's destruction. The cowardly general finally seeks refuge in the tent of

Heber, the Kenite. Heber's wife, Jael, deceives him with seeming welcome, then kills him brutally and efficiently.

The storyteller approves of Jael's action. We may find it repugnant, but people of that early time did not. A more important point is that Jael risked her own safety to help the people of God. For that she is praised.

The Kenites were nomads. They had allied themselves with the Canaanites, so Sisera had reason to assume he would be safe with them. Jael, however, had her own loyalties, and they lay with the God of Israel.

Barak originally gathered his troops at Kedesh in Naphtali near the Sea of Galilee. Here Heber's tent is near Kedesh by the oak of Zaanannim. It seems strange, though not impossible, that Sisera would flee into a major Israelite stronghold. Some suggest that there were two Kedeshes. If so, Heber would be living near a town to the north of Naphtali's territory.

Kishon is a two-forked stream running from the hills to the Mediterranean Sea. One fork comes from the Mount Tabor area; the other passes by Megiddo and Tanaach.

Sisera asks for water, but Jael gives him goat's milk instead. She may have had a purpose: Some goats' milk has a tranquilizing effect which she could use to dope her victim.

It would be very difficult to drive a tent peg through someone's skull. However, you could kill a sleeping man by driving the peg through the upper neck behind the lower jaw or at the back of the head at the spinal cord.

The Song of Deborah (5:1-31)

This is one of the oldest pieces of literature in the Old Testament. It is a poem, and contains a good deal of imagery plus many repetitions and parallel constructions designed for artistic effect. The writer has surrounded the poem with a little prose frame consisting of verse 1 and the last line of verse 31.

Who composed this song? Verse 1 suggests that

Deborah and Barak did. However, by verse 7 the poet is speaking to Deborah, so she cannot be the speaker. It is, of course, likely that Deborah and Barak did give some kind of victory speech after the battle. And it is possible that a portion of their words is preserved in verse 2. The rest of the poem could have been composed by an anonymous poet to fully celebrate the great deeds done through these judges.

After a call for everyone's attention (including the attention of even the greatest), the poem begins. It reminds listeners first of God's power and mighty saving acts in the Exodus and the conquest. Then it goes on to recount the story of Deborah and Barak. The story is similar to that told in Chapter 4, but does contain a few variations. (See Structure section in the introduction.)

One variation is in the space devoted to the tribes that fought. In Chapter 4 only Naphtali and Zebulun appear. Here each tribe, except Judah, is listed and judged as to whether or not it contributed to the common good. Those who helped receive praise; those who did not receive censure. This section shows the deep need for cooperation among the loosely organized tribes. It also shows that that cooperation was not always there. It is perhaps natural that those tribes who gave the most lived in the oppressed area, while those who helped least lived farther away.

As in the previous version, the writer is careful to note that Israel fought, but God won the battle. Here we see God using the forces of nature—power of the stars, rain, a flood—to enmire Sisera's chariots and defeat him.

The poet punctuates the story of Sisera's assassination with the picture of his mother's hopeless wait. The writer seems to take pleasure in her agony. Again our ancient Hebrews are not charitable. Yet gloating over an enemy's suffering may be understandable among a people regularly threatened by brutal oppression.

Seir is the chief mountain range of Edom.

The poet depicts God's power by picturing him as a colossus whose marching footsteps shake the earth and whose might disturbs all nature (*the earth trembled,* verse 4).

Shamgar is a judge mentioned briefly in Judges 3:31.

Caravans and peasantry ceased: Northern Israel was unsafe for travelers and even for farmers.

Verse 8 indicates that Israel was very short on weapons.

Deborah's method of arousing fervor for battle was a common one: Sing the old victory songs.

Machir is western Manasseh.

Unlike the prose version, we find here no mention of Jabin. The poem has as enemies only an anonymous group of Canaanite kings led by Sisera.

The *Kishon* is a two-forked stream flowing to the Mediterranean. In this version the battle takes place on the fork that flows by Taanach and Megiddo. This is south of Chapter 4's Mount Tabor locale.

Meroz is an unknown place or group.

§ § § § § § §

The Message of Judges 4–5

This passage carries the usual Deuteronomic message that God is powerful and will save if Israel will trust and obey. It also emphasizes two additional, though not unique, messages: (1) the importance of cooperation among God's people, and (2) the praiseworthiness of courage in carrying out God's will.

We, like the people of ancient Israel, need to rely on God's power if we are to succeed. On the other hand, we must recognize that courageous action on our part may be needed to implement God's plan for helping us.

§ § § § § § §

PART
ELEVEN Judges 6–8

Introduction to These Chapters

These are the stories of Gideon. Like many other
Israelite judges, Gideon is a great military leader. But in
other ways he is a different kind of judge. He does not
exemplify the faithful, courageous servant of God. He
comes from a Baal-worshiping family and town, he is
reluctant to accept God's call, he questions God's
concern, and he is slow to believe God's promises. Later
he proves headstrong, overly aggressive, and
self-serving. He recognizes that God alone must be king,
yet sets himself up as a formal leader. His work does
save Israel, but others of his actions set Israel up for
further disaster. As a judge Gideon is not an unqualified
success.

Time

Archeological findings place Gideon about fifty years
before Deborah, that is, around 1175 B.C. The final editor
may have been unaware that the stories were out of
order. Some commentators, however, see an alternating
pattern of good and not-so-good judges within the book
as a whole. This could explain Gideon's appearance after
Deborah.

Many of these stories show signs of great antiquity.
Though they have been passed down and edited over
generations, some of the materials may carry surprisingly
accurate reflections of the conditions and events they
describe.

Place
These stories center in the territory of Manasseh in northern Palestine.

The Enemy
The enemy in these stories is Midian, a nomadic tribe based east of the Jordan. Allied with Midian are Amalekite nomads and possibly others.

Structure
This is a series of stories joined together to form a continuous narrative. There are at least two strands of traditions here. The strands are so thoroughly mingled, however, that one cannot untangle them with any certainty; they may account for the varying descriptions we find of Gideon's character. At one time he is timid, at another extremely aggressive. Sometimes he is faithful and obedient to God; at other times he questions or ignores God. Some of the early stories are very hero-oriented. Other stories emphasize God's action, with Gideon as God's instrument.

Apparently all the storytellers did not hold the same picture of Gideon, nor did they have the same point to make. The final editor has taken care to use the stories to show the importance of recognizing God's kingship and saving power.

Here is an outline of these chapters.
I. Problems With the Midianites (6:1-6)
II. Gideon's Call (6:7-32)
III. Invasion and Uncertainty (6:33-40)
IV. Preparations (7:1-15)
V. Attack and Victory (7:16–8:21)
VI. The Story Ends (8:22-35)

Problems With the Midianites (6:1-6)

The story begins with the usual Deuteronomic formula: Israel has done evil, and that evil has brought oppression upon the people. A nomadic enemy has been making swift and frequent attacks, destroying crops and livestock so that Israel faces a severe food shortage. This enemy has a new and awesome weapon: the camel. The people of Israel are so powerless and so frightened that they hide in caves. Finally in their distress they turn to the God whom they had ignored.

The *Midianites* were a nomadic people living east of the Jordan and well to the south. They were perhaps better organized than most nomads, as they had kings. With Amalekites and similar tribes, the Midianites frequently raided Israel.

The *Amalekites* were a nomadic group that ranged over much of Palestine.

People of the East are miscellaneous tribes from east of the Jordan.

Gaza is a city in southern Palestine near the Mediterranean Sea. The Midianites apparently terrorized all of Palestine at this time.

Gideon's Call (6:7-32)

This section contains two stories: (1) Gideon's encounter with the angel, and (2) Gideon's call to destroy the Baal altar. In the first story God speaks mainly through a messenger. At the end of that story, however, and throughout the next story, God speaks directly to Gideon. The author may have used this device to emphasize Gideon's original distance from God and his growing ability to hear God's voice.

When the angel tells Gideon that God wants him to lead Israel out of oppression, Gideon's response is not one of great faith. First he questions that God even cares for Israel, then he argues that God's plan is senseless, since he and his clan are relatively weak. This is, of course, one reason God has chosen Gideon. Victory from such weakness will make it very clear that the conquering power is actually God's.

The presence of a Baal altar in Gideon's family indicates how pervasive idolatry has become. Family and neighbors alike have turned to Baal. There is no indication that Gideon has previously objected to this.

The name *Gideon* means *hacker*.

Ophrah, Gideon's home, was a town somewhere in Manasseh. Its exact location is unknown. Another Ophrah is in Benjamin.

The oak may have been a place where Baal oracles were given. The angel, however, takes it over for his own purposes.

Gideon has to thresh his wheat at night in a hidden wine press to avoid having it stolen.

An *ephah* is a measure frequently taken as two-thirds of a bushel or more. This would make a lot of bread! It is possible, however, that the ephah varied widely over the centuries and some smaller amount is meant.

Gideon, still not sure about this message, asks God to *show me a sign*.

Miraculous burning of the sacrificial food finally convinces Gideon of God's presence.

Asherah is one form of the name of a Semitic goddess. Here, however, it probably signifies a cult object or objects used in her worship.

By night (verse 2): Perhaps Gideon hopes no one will know who has vandalized the altar.

Joash defends his son by questioning Baal's power. Apparently his loyalty to Baal is not strong.

Jerubaal means *hacker of Baal* or *Let Baal bring suit*. The writer suggests that Gideon's alternate name came from his altar destruction. However, it is possible that Jerubaal was Gideon's original name. The ending could indicate a person whose god was Baal. The writer would want to explain why one of God's chosen judges should have such a name. This story would give him such an explanation.

Invasion and Uncertainty (6:33-40)

Another Midianite attack! This time they are taking over the Valley of Jezreel, a very fruitful area in the north. Gideon calls men from his own clan and tribe, then sends out an appeal to Asher, Zebulun, and Naphtali. As we shall see, this is more than God had in mind.

Gideon still has doubts, however. He asks God for yet another sign, using a fleece. A fleece placed on a warm rock at evening could generate considerable condensation, even though there was little dew elsewhere. So, the first test does not satisfy Gideon. He tries again. To keep the fleece dry while all around is wet would indeed be a miracle. God, of course, is able to provide such a miracle.

Preparations (7:1-15)

This section contains two more stories. The first is the testing and reduction of Gideon's army. Gideon has massed a huge force. But God wants no doubt left as to whose power won the victory. Gideon must win with only a few men and the might of God.

The second story again shows Gideon's uncertainty. Overhearing a Midianite soldier's account of a dream reassures him, however.

Harod's spring is a spot just south of the Midianite camp.

Mount Moreh is a hill across the valley from Mount Gilboa.

God sifts the soldiers by two tests: outright acknowledgement of fear and the drinking test. Those who knelt down to drink were vulnerable to attack because they weren't watching for the enemy. The others lifted the water in their hands and lapped it. They could still see who was coming. Fearless and alert men would certainly make preferable soldiers.

Jars may be *provisions* instead. However, jars or jugs figure prominently in the upcoming battle.

Cake of barley bread is the symbol for the Israelite farmers in the soldier's dream.

Attack and Victory (7:16–8:21)

This will be God's victory, not Gideon's. The main battle, in fact, will not be won by military strength at all, but by a God-directed trick. Moving at night, Israel simulates a three-sided attack. The surprise alone routs the Midianites. Neither Gideon nor the soldiers can say that their strength overcame the foe.

The remaining parts of the story show Gideon as a military hero pursuing and defeating the Midianites. God figures very little in these stories. Such a contrast with the previous one suggests a different storyteller.

After the initial rout, Gideon calls other tribes to help wipe out the retreating Midianites. The tribe of Ephraim, however, is displeased because it did not get to participate in the battle. Perhaps this is a matter of honor, perhaps a matter of shares in the spoil. Anyway, Gideon mollifies the group.

Next Gideon goes far beyond his original assignment. He chases his foe across the Jordan. There he approaches two cities of his own tribe, but they refuse to aid him. They live too close to the Midianites' home base to risk the foe's displeasure. Again we see the lack of cooperation so common in this period. Gideon punishes these cities. Then he slaughters the two Midianite kings he has captured. Only now do we learn his real reason for pursuing them: They killed his brothers. The saving of Israel has turned into a matter of personal revenge.

Night guard duty is divided into three parts. The

middle watch is the time during the middle of the night.

Zeperah is probably Zarethan in the Jordan Valley.

Abelmeholah and Tabbath are areas in the highlands across the Jordan.

The location of *Beth-barah* is unknown.

Gleaning of Ephraim is the mop-up work, finishing off the fleeing enemy.

Succoth is a rural rallying place located somewhere east of the Jordan.

Penuel is a city on the Jabbok east of the Jordan. This is the site of Jacob's struggle with the angel (Genesis 32:24-32).

Karkor is a spot well east of the Dead Sea near the Midianite home base. Gideon covers a bit of territory to catch those kings!

The location of *Heres Pass* is unknown.

The Story Ends (8:22-35)

Impressed by Gideon's feats, the people ask him to rule as king. Gideon refuses, saying that God is Israel's ruler. However, Gideon then turns around and asks for gold from the booty to make an ephod. This priestly vestment had attached to it the breastplate of judgment. It was not only a magnificent garment; it was a symbol of authority, a symbol of the judge. Gideon may not be king, but he is pushing as close to kingship as he can get. Gideon is flirting with God's own place of authority.

The conflict between grasping and refusing power may have been Gideon's own, or it may reflect two writers' views of this great hero. The story's final version stresses the importance of recognizing God's supreme authority by noting that the ephod soon becomes an idol in itself and leads to the downfall of Gideon's family.

Verses 29 to 31 form a bridge to the story of Gideon's son, Abimelech. His life will carry his father's mistakes further. *Abimelech*, significantly, means *my father is king*.

The story ends on a tragic note. The judge, Gideon,

has proved God's power. Yet Gideon's personal imperfection, his self-glorification, leads Israel back to a life of sin.

Ishmaelites is probably a generic term for nomad, rather than a more specific reference to descendants of Abraham's son, Ishmael.

Seventy sons is probably not a specific count of Gideon's offspring. Seventy was a politically significant number, indicating a full council.

Shechem was a Canaanite city and Baal cult center. Gideon's relationship with a Shechemite woman foreshadows Israel's trend back to idolatry.

§ § § § § § §

The Message of Judges 6–8

This section's major message is the basic Deuternomic
theme: God is the supreme authority, God is powerful,
and God will save if the people will trust and obey. The
story offers both a positive example (God's victory over
Midian) and a negative example (the eventual ruin that
came from Gideon's and Israel's failure to keep God in
the place of honor).

There is another message, however, that is not stated
directly. That is the idea that God can use not just good
people but badly flawed ones as well. Gideon was
originally fearful, lacking in faith, and doubtful that God
even cared. Later he overstepped his commission and
grasped at authority beyond his right. Yet God had used
Gideon to save Israel.

With all our scientific accomplishments, it is easy for
modern people to forget that it is not our own cleverness
but the power of God that saves and sustains us. God is
the world's supreme authority. Human attempts to usurp
that authority can only lead us to disaster. Nevertheless,
God will work with us as we are, flaws and all. The story
of Gideon stands for us as an affirmation of God's
powerful goodness and as a warning against the
temptation of self-glorification.

§ § § § § § §

Judges 9

Introduction to This Chapter

This story is different from most others in the book in that it is not a story about a judge. This is the story of a man who would lead, not by God's appointment, but at his own initiative. It is the story of Abimelech, Gideon's son. Gideon had refused the people's offer to crown him king. Abimelech was not so scrupulous. Although God was supposed to be Israel's only ruler, Abimelech set out to become a king. Abimelech was usurping God's authority, and he reaped a tragic harvest for his sin.

The story takes place in and around Shechem. Abimelech's mother was a Shechemite, so this was Abimelech's birthplace. It had a large Canaanite population and was an important center for Baal worship.

Shechem was centrally located in northern Israel and sat at the pass between Mount Ebal and Mount Gerizim. That made it an excellent place to establish a city-state. From there one could extend power in several directions. Abimelech may have had grand plans for an ever-enlarging kingdom.

Abimelech's lunge for power probably took place sometime between 1175 and 1150 B.C. We do not know when the original stories were first composed, but they could be quite old. Scholars can detect at least two strands of tradition within the present story, but the strands are thoroughly tied together now. The story probably appeared in the seventh-century Deuteronomic history. From there it would take its place in the post-exilic history that we have today.

Chapter 9 does not begin with the usual formula (*the people of Israel did what was evil in the sight of the* LORD *... the people cried ... and the* LORD *sent a deliverer*). The evil is obvious, but here there is no deliverer, so the formula would not fit. The story does support Deuteronomic attitudes and goals, however. The writer is openly contemptuous of Abimelech and carefully points out both his sins and his punishment.

Here is an outline of this chapter.

I. King of Shechem (9:1-6)
II. Jotham's Fable (9:7-21)
III. Quarrel and Rebellion (9:22-41)
IV. The Outcome (9:42-57)

King of Shechem (9:1-6)

Abimelech's first move is to approach his mother's family. He asks their help in promoting his campaign for kingship of Shechem. He then takes his pitch to the city fathers. There is no evidence that Abimelech's half-brothers live in Shechem or have any royal designs. But Abimelech offers the men of Shechem a choice between himself, with his Shechemite heritage, and all seventy of Gideon's sons as rulers. Given this somewhat dubious choice, the elders choose Abimelech. They bankroll him from the temple treasury. He hires a crew of thugs, then sets out to eliminate his "competition." He kills all his brothers except Jotham, who hides. Then he returns to be crowned king of Shechem.

The name *Abimelech* means *My father is king*. Gideon, a great military leader, was offered a kingship, but declined. He did, however, exercise extensive power and authority without the kingly title.

Jerubaal is Gideon's other name.

Baal–berith is lord of the covenant, a Canaanite god.

Scholars disagree on whether Beth-millo (verse 6) was an adjacent town, a place somehow related to Shechem's army, a fortress, or a pagan temple.

Jotham's Fable (9:7-21)

After the coronation, the remaining brother, Jotham, takes a prominent position on Mount Gerizim and delivers a speech. He tells a fable in which the trees have decided to choose a king. One by one the nominees decline. Each has a more important role to play in the community. Finally they ask the bramble, who accepts. The story is obviously meant to parallel Shechem's choice of Abimelech. So Jotham concludes with a warning to the people of Shechem: If they have dealt in good faith with Abimelech and with his father's house, then all should go well; if not, may they and Abimelech destroy each other. With that, Jotham flees. His words, however, will soon come tragically true.

There are complex translation problems here. Jotham was probably not on the actual mountain top, but on a prominent ledge part-way up. Archeologists have found evidence of a non-Baalite gathering place on such a ledge.

Jotham's tree-symbol for Abimelech is the bramble, the only tree with nothing worthwhile to give. It does offer the others shade (protection), but what kind of shade can a bramble give to large trees? His promises are worthless! What's more, in a hot, dry place fire can break out in a bramble patch and spread to destroy even great cedars. This is the kind of "protection" Jotham predicts Abimelech will provide.

The men of Shechem have already paid for a massive slaughter of Jerubaal's (Gideon's) sons (*dealt well with Jerubaal*, verse 16). This is how they have treated the family of a man who saved them from Midianite oppression. What they deserve is obvious.

The location of *Beer* is unknown.

Quarrel and Rebellion (9:22-41)

As so often happens, a relationship begun in treachery turns sour. The editor sees this as God's way of punishing all parties concerned.

Abimelech is living in Arumah, southeast of Shechem. Zebul serves as his deputy in the city. From Zebul Abimelech learns that public opinion is turning against him. The people are robbing travelers on the highway. This may be depriving Abimelech of lucrative turnpike or protection fees. The Shechemites have also set up an ambush for Abimelech himself. Soon an opportunist named Gaal has gained a following and plans a coup.

Zebul and Abimelech foil Gaal, however. Zebul maneuvers Gaal to the city gates. There he must face Abimelech and his army unprepared. Gaal flees, never to return.

Saying that Abimelech *ruled over Israel* is an overstatement. He ruled only the small area around Shechem.

An *evil spirit* means bad feelings.

Little is known about Gaal. His name, however, combines elements meaning *to loathe* and *slave*. His father was an adherent of the corrupt temple in Shechem. From Israel's point of view Gaal would be a poor candidate for kingship.

Gaal compares Abimelech's mixed parentage (*Who is Abimelech?* verse 28) with his own pure Shechemite line as a way to gain leverage with the city elders.

The Hebrew word for *center of the land* means *navel*. This is a spot on Mount Gerizim thought to be the earth's center, the place where heaven and earth meet.

The Outcome (9:42-57)

The day after Gaal's defeat, Abimelech returns to Shechem. He slaughters a number of citizens in the fields, then destroys the city. From there he goes on to the town of Thebez, where he wreaks further destruction.

He begins to burn the fortress tower as he has the one at Shechem, but this time a woman in the tower heaves out a millstone. The stone hits Abimelech, crushing his skull. The story ends with an editorial note that by their mutual destruction God has requited all the crimes of Abimelech and the men of Shechem.

The act of sowing with salt was intended to make the city perpetually desolate. The idea probably comes from the fact that nothing can grow in salted ground. The act may also be a symbolic implementation of a covenantal curse. If so, Abimelech is again pre-empting God's authority by doing this on his own.

El-berith is a variation of Baal-berith. The house of El-berith was apparently a temple that included a fortress-tower. This tower may have been outside the town, although that would be unusual.

The location of *Mount Zalmon* is uncertain, but it might be another name for Mount Ebal.

Thebez is a town about twelve miles northeast of Shechem. Possibly it had cooperated in Shechem's revolt against Abimelech.

A *millstone* is a large grinding stone. It would normally be too heavy for one person to lift. The woman may have had help getting it out the window.

Abimelech asks his armor-bearer to run him through with a sword so he will not die in disgrace, killed by a woman.

§ § § § § § §

The Message of Judges 9

Throughout the Book of Judges the main message has been that those who trust and obey God, who affirm God's authority, will remain safe and prosperous. Here we see the negative side of that message. The writer presents Abimelech as a bad example. This young man has grasped at power, power that only God may exercise or confer. For this and related sins, Abimelech dies.

In today's technologically advanced, scientifically minded world, many people find it hard to recognize God's activity. It is easy to assume that we are in charge of things. Forgetting that this is God's world, we begin to make our own rules and behave however we choose toward other people and toward the environment. When we do this we can reap only disaster. No one—not Abimelech, not his modern counterparts—can get away with usurping God's authority.

§ § § § § § §

Judges 10–12

Introduction to These Chapters

Here we find accounts of six lesser-known judges. The Deuteronomic editor apparently knew very little about these men. Perhaps few significant events occurred in their times. The story of just one, Jephthah, is told in detail. He is the only one who faced and put down oppression. The others ruled in peace, apparently serving mainly as administrators. They saved Israel, not from outside evil, but from internal disorder.

These judges served after the death of Abimelech. We can't date Abimelech's "reign" precisely, so we can't know exactly when these six judges lived. It was probably around the middle of the 12th century B.C.

These chapters contain a mixture of old stories, historical notes, and editorial comments. The notes about five of the judges are very short. There is no mention of the people doing evil or of any oppression. The usual opening and closing formulas are absent. Those formulas do occur, however, in the Jephthah story. There we see again that *the people of Israel did what was evil in the sight of the Lord . . . the anger of the Lord was kindled against them . . . and the people cried to the Lord.* When they did, Jephthah was available to help them.

Here is an outline of these chapters:
I. Tola (10:1-2)
II. Jair (10:3-5)
III. Jephthah (10:6–12:7)
IV. Ibzan (12:8-10)
V. Elon (12:11-12)
VI. Abdon (12:13-15)

Tola (10:1-2)

Tola receives only this brief note in the Book of Judges.
Apparently he did nothing spectacular. Still, he was
remembered over the centuries for his long and effective
administration. Israel presumably remained at peace
throughout his career. His home, Shamir, is probably a
variant of Samaria.

Jair (10:3-5)

Another brief note tells of Jair. This judge, too, gave
Israel peaceful administration. Jair was a judge on the
east side of Jordan—he lived in Gilead, in the eastern
territory of Manasseh, about 10-16 miles southeast of the
Sea of Galilee.

Thirty sons and thirty cities suggest that Jair held
extensive administrative responsibilities. The sons may be
offspring or they may be chieftains under Jair's direction.

Thirty asses are an indication of prosperity.

Kamon is a town east of the Jordan on the road to Irbid.

Jephthah (10:6–12:7)

Jephthah was also from Gilead on the east side of the
Jordan. He is the only judge of this group who was a
military leader. He was, however, a man who tried to use
diplomacy before war. He was also a man who kept his
word, no matter what the cost.

These chapters include several stories and editorial
notes tied together to make a continuous narrative. They

begin with the classic formula, *and the people again did what was evil*. . . . Then we find a list of enemies and enemy gods. The whole list does not really apply to Jephthah's time. It is a summary of Israel's major enemies over a long period, both before and after Jephthah. The writer seems to be saying that any time powerful peoples threatened Israel, the Israelites were tempted to worship the enemies' gods.

When we actually get into Jephthah's story we find that oppression is coming from the Ammonites. These Ammonites were relative latecomers to the area. Sometime after Israel's settlement, the Ammonites had taken over the old Moabite territory far to the east of the Jordan. Now they were moving west into Israel's territory along the east bank of the Jordan and even into Israel's lands across the river.

Finally the people of Israel recognize their sin and cry to God for help. God expresses anger, but still cares. To show God's power and obvious concern, the writer lists the peoples from whom God has already saved Israel. This list again includes both past enemies and enemies who would not even arise until after Jephthah's time. But the point is made: God can and does save the people, yet the people lack both trust and gratitude. God suggests that the people should look for salvation to their new gods. But the people realize their error. So, God does save them.

The judge God uses is an unlikely candidate. In fact, it is embarrassing for the tribal leaders to ask his help. Jephthah, an illegitimate child, has been banished. He has to be brought back from another town. Jephthah agrees to take both military and civil leadership. God ratifies the agreement between Jephthah and his native tribe.

Jephthah first tries diplomacy with the Ammonites. He offers a reasoned argument for Israel's claim to the east bank territory. Israel had taken it centuries before from the Amorites. The Ammonites had not questioned this settlement for 300 years. Why should they start fighting over it now? Besides, the Ammonites already had ample territory to the east. Why not stay there in peace as their Moabite predecessors had?

The Ammonites do not accept Israel's argument, and war ensues. In preparing for battle, Jephthah makes a rash vow to God. He wins the fight. So, on his return home, he must fulfill his vow—he must sacrifice the first living thing that comes out of his house. That turns out to be his only child. True to his word, Jephthah does sacrifice her. The storyteller seems to both applaud Jephthah's integrity and mourn his tragedy. Human sacrifice was not acceptable in Israel, yet a vow to God was sacred. No one would dare trifle with the Deity by failing to honor a vow.

Next Jephthah, like Gideon before him, must deal with an angry group of Ephraimites. (See Judges 8:1-3.)

Jephthah has crossed the river into Ephraimite territory to clean out the Ammonites there. The Ephraimites claim they weren't informed or called to help; Jephthah says that he had asked for help earlier but the Ephraimites did not respond. Again Jephthah tries to argue his opponents out of fighting, but they refuse. A battle ensues, Israelite tribe against Israelite tribe. Jephthah overcomes the Ephraimites. As they try to flee back across the Jordan, Jephthah's men stop them. The Gileadites apply a test. Any man who claims he is not an Ephraimite must say the word "Shibboleth." If he cannot pronounce it correctly, he is proved an Ephraimite and must die. Thus the complaining Ephraimite band is virtually wiped out.

With peace finally established, Jephthah continues to administer the Gilead area until his death.

Gilead is a sub-group of the eastern Manasseh tribe.

The _Amorites_ are Canaanites. Some live in Judah; others live east of the Jordan.

The _Ammonites_ are an aggressive tribe living east of the Jordan.

Maon is a town in the hill district of southern Judah. Maonites could be Edomite inhabitants of this town, or they could be members of a larger confederation from the east to which Maon belonged. Maonites were prominent enemies of Israel at a much later time, around 873–849 B.C.

Sidonians are residents of a city on the Mediterranean. These, too, fought against Israel somewhat later.

Philistines are a group living along the Mediterranean coast. They appear prominently in the Samson and David stories.

Amalekites are nomads who roamed over much of Palestine, often collaborating with Israel's enemies.

Gilead was the father of Jephthah (11:1) may simply mean that Jephthah was a Gileadite. Or, it may suggest that the tribe was his father. In other words, his individual father was not known.

Tob is either a city in Syria or a town about fifteen miles east of Ramoth-gilead.

Three hundred years is a round number roughly indicating the whole period of the judges up to this time.

The coming of the *Spirit of the* LORD was the sign of a true judge.

Mizpah (verse 29) is not Mizpah of the west, but a town of unknown location in Gilead.

Whoever comes forth (verse 31) might also read *whatever comes forth*. Animals could be sheltered in Jephthah's house, and he could be assuming that some animal would wander out for his sacrifice.

Zaphon is near the east bank of the Jordan, probably between Succoth and Zarethan.

Ibzan (12:8-10)

No more than this is known of Ibzan. He apparently administered Israel in times of peace. The thirty sons suggest heavy administrative responsibilities. His ability to arrange so many marriages suggests that he had good relationships with neighboring tribes. Ibzan's home, Bethlehem, is a northern town in Zebulun, not the southern town of David and Jesus.

Elon (12:11-12)

Elon was also from Zebulun. The writer apparently had very little information about him. He, too, ruled in peace; at least, he fought no battles worth noting. His name means *oak* or *terebinth* (another large tree). Aijalon's location is uncertain. The name, however, could be an alternate spelling of Elon, so there could be some confusion here between the judge's name and his burial place.

Abdon (12:13-15)

This is another little-known judge who apparently ruled in peace. Pirathon was probably about six miles west of Shechem. Forty sons and thirty grandsons would make a standard council of seventy. This was a large clan for which Abdon was responsible. The seventy asses again suggest prosperity. Abdon could afford to provide donkeys for all his subordinates.

§ § § § § § §

The Message of Judges 10–12

The basic message of the Jephthah story is the familiar Judges theme: when people sin, they suffer; when they turn to God, God can and will save them. The message of the remaining notices is an implicit rather than an explicit variation of this basic theme. The brief notes with little comment suggest that during these years the people did not sin and thus were able to live peacefully under a God-given judge. These notes also suggest that good administration is a gift of God just as much as is a more dramatic military victory.

To us these passages may be saying that God provides for the chosen people in many ways. When necessary God may save us in a dramatic way from our enemies. At other times God may keep us safe by the gift of good, steady leadership. Whatever the situation, the blessings of safety, freedom, and peace come from a good, powerful, and caring God. They are available to us when we remain faithful and obedient.

§ § § § § § §

Judges 13–16

Introduction to These Chapters

These are the stories of Samson. Samson was a man chosen before birth to be God's instrument in freeing Israel. He was not what we would consider a perfect candidate. He was headstrong, hot-tempered, not very smart, and unwilling or unable to learn from his mistakes. He had a weakness for women and blundered into all sorts of trouble. Yet, in God's Spirit, this man had magnificent physical strength. God used that strength to subdue large numbers of the foreigners who were ruling over Israel.

The stories take place in Judah, in southern Dan, and in the southern Philistine territory near the Mediterranean Sea. Samson's home is on the border between Judah and Dan, about fourteen miles west of Jerusalem.

The enemy Israel faces is Philistia. The Philistines had entered Palestine around 1200 B.C. They had settled along the seacoast, then proceeded to push progressively inland. Slowly they inched ever farther into Israel's territory. By the time of Samson (1150–1100 B.C.) the Philistines had apparently moved into much of southern Palestine. At first they were not heavy-handedly oppressive, but in later years Israel would frequently have to fight off Philistine armies. The memory of these violent encounters may have added to the storytellers' obvious glee in relating their tales of Philistine defeat.

These chapters include several stories and even an ancient poem or victory song. Unlike some parts of

Judges, this section contains very little editorial comment. That may be because the stories were so old and so well known that they were set in the public mind. The editor would not then feel so free to add his own comments. The cycle does begin, however, with the standard Deuteronomic formula, *And the people of Israel again did what was evil in the sight of the Lord*. The rest of the formula, *the people cried . . . and the Lord raised up a judge*, is missing.

The incidents recorded here are excellent examples of ancient storytelling. They are highly entertaining, suspenseful, and skillfully constructed so that climactic events are set up in advance yet held back just enough to retain the listener's attention. As in most folk literature, we find here some very effective exaggeration. Samson's feats of strength and the number of Philistines killed are fantastic. Yet the exaggeration does not mean that the stories lack historical roots. It simply means that the storytellers playfully "poked their listeners in the ribs" a little to make the point stick.

Modern readers may be somewhat surprised to find here a biblical hero whose morals are distressingly low. Samson's visits to prostitutes and wanton murder of innocent men in Ashkelon do not match our expectations of a religious figure. What's more, the writers and editors do not criticize Samson's behavior. We must, however, consider the times in which Samson lived. Apparently this behavior was not unusual. And, because the stories were so firmly set, later editors neither condemned nor brushed up Samson's brutality and looseness. Instead they allowed his imperfections to focus the spotlight completely on God's power. In effect they said, "Here is a man in all his weakness. See how God has been able to use him."

Here is an outline of these chapters.

I. The Story Begins (13:1-25)
II. A Stormy Marriage (14:1–15:8)
III. Confrontation With the Philistines (15:9-20)
IV. Temptations, Defeat, and Victory (16:1-31)

The Story Begins (13:1-25)

The writer opens with his usual formula. Then he moves right into the ancient story.

An angel appears to a barren woman announcing that she will soon bear a son who will someday save Israel. The mother must observe strict prenatal instructions because this child is to be a Nazirite from conception. She must keep all the Nazirite rules to avoid compromising her child's purity. Her husband, Manoah, requests and receives additional verification of the message. Finally the son, Samson, is born. Very early God's Spirit (proof of divine election) stirs in the child.

Zorah is a town fourteen miles west of Jerusalem, on the border between Judah and Dan.

A *Nazirite* is a person consecrated to God for a period of time, not necessarily a lifetime. Later Nazirites kept three rules. They did not cut their hair, they abstained from wine and other alcoholic beverages, and they avoided contact with dead or unclean flesh. These are the rules given to Samson's mother. Other older accounts do not mention avoidance of the dead.

Manoah asks for verification because a woman's word is not considered reliable.

The angel's name is *wonderful*, beyond comprehension, as is his entire being.

Samson is a Canaanite name. The meaning of the name is unclear.

Mahanehdan is a camp of Dan.

Eshtaol is a town located about a mile from the village of Zorah.

A Stormy Marriage (14:1–15:8)

In this next story Samson is a young man. He is already quite headstrong. Hebrew parents usually chose their children's spouses. However, Samson has taken a shine to a Philistine girl from Timnah. He decides to marry her against his parents' wishes. They, of course, are concerned because she is not of their people and does not worship their God. She is, in fact, a member of the nation that is taking over Israel. Samson, however, goes ahead. He makes his own wedding arrangements. In one of the story's few editorial remarks (14:4), someone has explained this odd marriage as God's way of arranging a situation where Samson will get into a fight with the Philistines.

On a trip to Timnah we see the first sign of Samson's great strength. He tears a lion apart with his bare hands. On the next trip he finds honey in the carcass. That honey provides the lead-in to a riddle on which the rest of the story hangs.

Now the seven-day wedding feast begins. Samson makes a bet that that the guests cannot answer a riddle. On the fourth day the guests approach the bride for help in learning the answer. Her tears and pleading melt the foolish Samson. So, on the final feast day the guests spring their response. Samson must pay up.

But he does not have the sixty garments required. The marriage legalities are incomplete (all would be ratified at the end of the seventh day), but Samson angrily stomps off. He goes twenty miles to Ashkelon, kills thirty Philistines, and brings back two garments from each to give the guests. Then he leaves.

The bride's surprised and embarrassed parents promptly marry the girl to the best man. Some time later, Samson returns to find his bride married. In anger he burns the Philistines' crops. The Philistines take their vengeance on the bride's family. Samson retaliates with a huge slaughter. He then goes into hiding.

Timnah is a city on the northern border of Judah. It would be about four miles southwest of Mahanehdan.

Ashkelon is a Philistine town on the Mediterranean Sea.

The Israelites saw circumcision as a sign of their dedication to God. Philistines did not practice circumcision.

The honey may foreshadow Samson's role as a strong fighter. Mesopotamians used honey in preparation for battle. Israelites believed honey produced enlightenment and courage. Here, ironically, this very substance plays a major part in Samson's first downfall.

She wept seven days (verse 17) is an error. Obviously she wept only four of the seven days.

The bride's father tries vainly to placate this dangerous, angry man by offering him another daughter, a *younger sister.*

The *cleft of rock at Etam* is a hiding place in the rocks near Samson's home.

Confrontation With the Philistines (15:9-20)

The retaliatory cycle continues. The Philistines come after Samson. Fearing reprisals, the men of Judah determine to turn him over. He agrees, assuming that he can easily fight off the Philistines anyway. He meets them, snaps his bonds, grabs a handy jawbone, and uses it to kill a thousand men. Then this fearless fighter suddenly realizes that he is thirsty and grows afraid that he may be weakened. God, however, opens a rock where Samson finds water.

The bone and water incidents are two examples of a common type of biblical literature, the story that explains or is verbally connected with the name of a place.

Linguistic analysis indicates that Samson's song (verse 16) is a very ancient one.

Lehi means *jawbone.*

Three thousand are a lot of men. The Judahites had great respect for Samson's strength!

A *fresh jawbone* would be much stronger than a dry, brittle, old one.

Ramath-lehi means *height of the jawbone*. The battle took place on high ground.

En-hakkore means *mortar*. This was a hollow stone in the shape of a mortar. Water may have collected there, or the stone may have held a small spring. Water from a rock recalls a similar experience of Moses. (See Exodus 17.)

Temptations, Defeat, and Victory (16:1-31)

Here we find two more stories of Samson's prodigious strength.

First Samson goes off to the Philistine city of Gaza, where he visits a harlot. Realizing he is dangerous, the men of Gaza determine to capture him. Apparently, though, they fall asleep during the evening. At midnight Samson decides to leave the locked city. So, he pulls up the gates and carries them all the way to Hebron.

Next Samson goes to the Valley of Sorek, where he meets and moves in with Delilah. The Philistine men bribe her to learn the secret of Samson's strength. Delilah wheedles and nags at Samson. At first he puts her off with phony stories. But finally female pleas again undo him. Perhaps trusting too much in his physical strength, he tells her his strength lies in his hair. Actually, his special Nazirite commitment is the source of his strength. Cutting off the hair would end that commitment. And, without the commitment he would not have strength from God. But Samson may never have taken his Nazirite status seriously. He has ignored the prohibitions against strong drink and touching dead bodies already. (The last, however, may not have been a requirement in Samson's time.) Now Samson rather lightly breaks the last vow and, to his surprise, loses his strength. The Philistines bind and blind him.

Still, God is able to use Samson one last time. The Philistines, celebrating his capture, proceed to make great fun of him. In the intervening time, however, Samson's hair has been growing back. Samson calls upon God to strengthen him once more. Then, in God's Spirit, Samson pulls down the temple pillars, killing thousands of Philistines and himself. In death he is avenged.

Gaza is a Philistine city of southwest Palestine about thirty-eight miles south of Zorah.

Hebron is an Israelite city in southeast Palestine. It is thirty-eight miles east of Gaza.

The large metal *gate of the city* would be imbedded in stone posts with two-story guardhouses on either side. The Gazite men may have spent the night inside the guardhouses and so would not hear Samson soon enough to prevent his escape.

The *Valley of Sorek* is a grape-growing area near Zorah.

The name *Delilah* means *flirtatious*.

1,100 pieces of silver is a huge amount of money.

The strings of a loom are called a *web*.

Dagon is an ancient Mesopotamian god whose worship had spread into Palestine.

3,000 on the roof is the storyteller's exaggerated version of a great many people.

§ § § § § § §

The Message of Judges 13–16

The Samson stories provide yet another variation on the basic Deuteronomic message that God is the source of saving strength for Israel. Samson is not a hero in himself. In fact, on his own he is a bumbling, hot-tempered fool. Yet God can use a man like Samson to free the people.

The stories also illustrate a converse message. Breaking the covenant relationship with God cuts one off from God's strength. Samson, in allowing his hair to be cut, broke his Nazirite vow. He broke his relationship with God and lost the strength that came from God.

The story's dramatic ending offers another basic Deuteronomic message: When people turn and call upon God, God does come to them and save them.

Beneath the human interest and excitement of the Samson tales the writer has given us once again his essential theological word: If we remain in right relationship with God, God will strengthen and save us. If not, we will suffer. Modern people, as much as their ancient counterparts, need to recognize these basic truths if we, as individuals and as a race, are to survive.

§ § § § § § §

Judges 17–18

Introduction to These Chapters

These and the remaining chapters form a kind of
appendix to the Book of Judges. They are historical
reminiscences from the same general time period, but
they do not narrate stories of particular judges. The
stories lack the usual Deuteronomic formula. There is no
note of Israel's sin, of outside oppression, of a cry for
help, or of God's provision for a hero-judge to save the
people. These chapters are simply additional bits of
history that the editor apparently did not want to leave
out.

The story in Chapters 17–18 seems to have been
composed for a particular purpose: to explain why for
many years Levitical priests maintained an illegitimate
sanctuary in Dan. The story's development involves
events in the lives of a man from Ephraim, a Levite
from Judah, and a large portion of the tribe of Dan.
These three elements converge because of some religious
paraphernalia. As the tale unfolds, the Ephraimite sets
up a worship center and hires the Levite to tend it. At
that point, the Ephraimite loses the worship center to
thieving Danites, who are in the process of moving to
new territory. Like many portions of Judges, this is a
good example of ancient storytelling.

These events take place around 1100–1050 B.C. At that
time Philistine pressure was squeezing the Danites out of
their allotted territory. The religious and social situation
reflected here suggests that the story itself may come

from a time near the events described.

The story's age could help explain a factor that may seem odd to modern readers. That is the biblical storyteller's apparent unconcern for the morality (or immorality) of his characters. The story tells of theft, image-making (which is expressly forbidden and roundly criticized in other texts), and the slaughter of innocent people. The storyteller makes no explicit comment on any of this. Neither does any editor. Only the story itself and two brief bits of editorial information offer any possible hint of justice for these wrongs. Such an attitude could reflect the less-sensitive morality of an earlier age. By the time the editors incorporated this material it would be so entrenched in the popular mind that additional comment would be difficult, and perhaps unnecessary, to include.

On the surface, these chapters do little to promote the writer's particular theological concerns, but he apparently chose to preserve them, basically unaltered, as part of his people's heritage.

Here is an outline of these chapters.

I. Micah's Story (17:1-13)
II. The Danites' Move (18:1-13)
III. The Danites and Micah Clash (18:14-26)
IV. Settlement at Laish (18:27-31)

Micah's Story (17:1-13)

As the story begins, an Ephraimite, Micah, has stolen 1,100 pieces of silver from his mother. Possibly because he is frightened by the curse she has put on the silver, Micah confesses and returns the money to her. His mother consecrates the silver to make images for the worship of God. Micah sets up a shrine, with his son as priest.

Some time later, a Levite who is looking for work comes by. Micah hires him to replace the son as priest.

He hopes that having a "real" priest will improve his fortunes.

Micah is not the later prophet Micah. Rather, this Micah is an otherwise unknown man from the tribe of Ephraim. The name Micah is short for Micayehu, which means *who is like or comparable to Yahweh (God)?* Later listeners would probably catch an ironic contrast between this man's pious name and his questionable religious and moral life.

Ephraim is a tribe located in the central part of Palestine, north of Judah and north of Dan's original territory.

1,100 pieces of silver is a great deal of money. Each of the Philistine men offered Delilah this amount to betray Samson (Judges 16:5).

It is unclear at first whether the *graven image, molten image* is one molded and engraved image or two images. In 18:17, however, there are clearly two images. These were not pagan idols but images intended for the worship of God, although Exodus 20:4 forbids any kind of image.

An *ephod* is a religious vestment worn during religious ceremonies.

Teraphim are small idols. The Babylonians used these to foretell events or to discern the will of the gods. This seems to have been one function of Micah's shrine. (See 18:5-6.)

The comment that there was *no king* underscores Israel's loose organization at this time. There was no one in authority who was empowered to make nationwide rules, so each one had to make his own. Micah and the Levite obviously did so.

Levites were normally members of the tribe of Levi, who were set aside to serve as priests. They did not receive a particular territorial allotment, but were assigned certain cities scattered throughout Palestine (Joshua 21). *Levites* may sometimes, however, have designated a person who served as a priest but was a member of another tribe. This might explain the strange description of a Levite of the *family of Judah*. Another possibility is that the author meant simply that this Levite had been living in Judah. We do not know why this Levite was looking for another place to work. Perhaps there were too many Levites in Bethlehem, or perhaps he simply wanted a change.

The Danites' Move (18:1-13)

Now we turn to a seemingly unrelated situation. Dan has been assigned land between Judah and Ephraim (Joshua 19:40-46). The tribe has not been strong enough to hold this land, however, so the group decides to move. Five spies travel north looking for a spot. On the way, these spies stop at Micah's house. They ask the Levite for a sign concerning their mission. The Levite assures them that God is with them. At Laish they find a peaceful, prosperous, and defenseless people. Most of the people of Dan then set out to take this area. As they travel north, the whole group stops at Micah's house.

In biblical Hebrew, the name *Dan* means *judgment*. Unknowingly, the tribe of Dan does visit judgment upon Micah. But the writer does not make an explicit point of this outcome.

Zorah and *Eshtaol* are two towns on the border between Dan and Judah. Over the years there was some confusion as to which tribe held them. In Joshua 15:33 the towns are assigned to Judah. Zorah is noted as the home of Samson (Judges 13:2).

Recognized the voice (verse 3): Perhaps they recognized the Levite's accent or realized there was a Levite about when they heard him chanting.

Laish is a city about 100 miles north of Micah's home. The name means *lion*.

Sidonians were inhabitants of Sidon, a Phoenician city on the Mediterranean. The people of Laish were of

Phoenician stock but, living so far inland, they were isolated from their relatives. Thus, they would receive no help from outside.

Kiriath-jearim is a town about 8 miles northwest of Jerusalem.

Mahanehdan is a camp of the tribe of Dan. In this story it is at Kiriath-jearim. As a camp, however, it may have moved around. It is not necessarily in the same location as the camp mentioned in the Samson story (Judges 13:25).

The Danites and Micah Clash (18:14-26)

The Danite spies, remembering Micah's shrine, suggest that the tribe take his religious equipment. The tribe agrees. The spies also convince the Levite to come with them by offering him a job promotion. Now he can be priest to a whole tribe, not just one family or village. Micah tries to recover his gods, but the Danites are too strong for him.

The Levite's character is rather interesting—he will apparently do anything to get ahead. But the storyteller makes no point of this nor does any later editor. Perhaps they expect the listener's own sense of right and wrong to provide judgment.

The point of putting the *little ones . . . in front* is to put the warriors in back to protect both families and images from a rear attack by Micah.

Settlement at Laish (18:27-31)

The Danites attack Laish without warning, slaughtering its unsuspecting inhabitants. Then they rebuild the city and rename it Dan. They set up a sanctuary with Micah's images and install the Levite to preside over it. Thus the story ends.

Apparently tradition held that the priests at Dan were descendants of Moses' grandson, Jonathan. The text seems to say that the previously unidentified Levite was actually this Jonathan.

Captivity of the land means either the Assyrian conquest of 733 B.C. or the forced removal of the Danites from the area in 721 B.C. The point is just a small historical note, with no comment or criticism attached. The fact could, however, suggest to later listeners a punishment for Danite sin.

Shiloh is a city in Ephraim located about ten miles northeast of Bethel. For many years Shiloh housed a major Israelite temple. That temple was destroyed about 1060 B.C.

§ § § § § § §

The Message of Judges 17–18

Actually, this story carries no explicit message. Listeners or readers are left to determine the meaning for themselves. Listeners of a later time would probably take an "isn't it too bad?" attitude toward the setting up of images and independent sanctuaries. Yet, there are only two historical notes that might vaguely suggest editorial disapproval.

The story does, however, imply a basic Deuteronomic message. The message is that the person who sins will eventually suffer. That is clearly what happens in Micah's case. He originally steals some silver. In the end, his silver idols are stolen from him. The case of the Danites is not so certain. It depends on whether or not that brief mention of the "captivity" was meant to suggest a punishment.

The modern reader can perhaps take from Judges 17–18 this thought: that evil tends to bring evil back to the perpetrator. Recompense may not always be immediate or obvious, but wrong actions set in motion other wrongs that can eventually come back to us.

§ § § § § § §

Judges 19–21

Introduction to These Chapters

This section, along with Chapters 17–18, forms an
appendix to the Book of Judges. The story belongs to the
Judges time period. This is not, however, the story of a
judge. It is the story of an evil event that led to civil war
and the near devastation of the tribe of Benjamin. Even
though it is not the usual "judge" story, the writer has
apparently preserved this account in order to offer as
complete an historical record as possible.

These chapters include several distinct traditions and
editorial notes. In some spots we can see that a later
editor or storyteller needed to give his listeners extra
information to explain points of a very old tale. The final
editor, however, has skillfully woven the parts together to
form an exciting and coherent narrative.

The story lacks the usual Deuteronomic formula noting
Israel's sin, the oppression it brought, Israel's cry for
help, and God's gift of a judge. This standard structure
would not fit the situation at all. Instead, it begins and
ends with the simple comment, *In those days there was no
king in Israel.*

We do find here, as in many ancient tales, some skillful
storytelling techniques, including occasional exaggeration
for effect. Still, much of this material deals with a real
historical event. Certainly the story accurately depicts
Israel's political situation at the time. We see here a
leaderless people divided, tribe against tribe, trying to
wrestle with major problems of justice, order, and unity.

Mob action, unaided by previously formed policies or institutions, leads Israel to the brink of disaster.

The story, ancient and reworked as it is, offers a curious mix of moral attitudes. The lack of hospitality, the threat of homosexual attack on a guest, the gang rape and murder receive the label "abomination." The authors and editors, however, say nothing about the offering of two women to placate the mob, the slaughter of women and children in Jabesh-gilead, or the kidnapping of wives for the Benjaminites. We would hesitate to draw conclusions about Israel's morality from this story, except to say that it offers an interesting peek into the development of moral sensitivity. Later editors' hesitation to change or comment on the story does not necessarily mean that they shared the story's earlier attitudes.

Here is an outline of these chapters.

I. The Levite's Story (19:1-30)
II. Israel's Response (20:1-48)
III. Making Peace Again (21:1-25)

The Levite's Story (19:1-30)

The story begins with a common Judges formula noting that *In those days . . . there was no king in Israel.* This simple statement places the events in the time before the monarchy. It may also, however, be meant to convey the tragedy of Israel's anarchic situation and/or the idea that in those days God alone was king. In any case, this opening effectively suggests the kind of inter-tribal chaos we will soon see in detail.

We next learn of an unnamed Levite who is returning with his concubine from Judah to his home in Ephraim. Late in the afternoon he reaches Jerusalem, where his servant suggests they spend the night. Ironically the Levite refuses because this is a foreign city. (Israel did not control Jerusalem until much later.) He prefers to go on to Gibeah in Benjamin where he expects greater hospitality among Israelites. Unfortunately he will receive there worse treatment than any foreigners would be likely to give.

In Gibeah there are no hotels, yet no one will take the Levite in, even though his servant, donkeys, and goods indicate his prosperity. Finally an old Ephraimite living in the town extends an invitation. Soon, however, some of the Gibeonite men arrive, demanding the Levite as an object for attack. The Ephraimite, determined to protect his guest, offers the men both the Levite's concubine and his own virgin daughter. The men refuse. Finally, however, the Levite pushes the concubine out and the men spend the night raping her.

By morning the woman is dead. The Levite carries her body home, cuts it into twelve pieces, and sends the pieces out among the twelve tribes of Israel.

A *Levite* is a priest, a member of the tribe of Levi. This tribe had no territorial claim but lived in cities throughout Palestine.

To *sojourn* means to stay for a time. A sojourner was a person who lived among people not of his or her own tribe.

A *concubine* is a slave purchased as a wife.

Jebus is another name for Jerusalem. It lies five to six miles north of Bethlehem.

Gibeah is a town in Benjamin four miles north of Jerusalem. At the time of this story Gibeah was surrounded by Canaanite settlements. Canaanite influence may have led to the Gibeonites' abominable behavior.

Ramah is a town about six miles north of Jerusalem.

Throughout the Middle East, hospitality to a traveler was a sacred duty. In Gibeah, however, no Benjaminite would invite the Levite in. Only a man from Ephraim would offer him the customary politeness.

To *know him* means to have sexual intercourse with him. For a similar situation see the attack on Lot's guests at Sodom (Genesis 19).

The guest-host relationship was a sacred one. The host was to ensure the guest's safety and well-being; the guest was bound to do no harm to the host. If the Gibeonite men were to succeed in their plans, the host would be gravely at fault for failing to protect his guest.

The offer of his daughter and the concubine is the Ephraimite's last wild attempt to avoid the sin of failing to protect a guest. Women, even women one cared for very much, were dispensable. The Levite, however, finally prevents harm to his host's child by shoving his concubine out to the men.

Sent her throughout the territory (verse 29): An animal cut in pieces was a signal used to mobilize the tribes for a fight.

Israel's Response (20:1-48)

An army assembles. The Levite tells his story, with slight alterations to put his own part in the best light. The Israelites, enraged by the Gibeonite crime, seek revenge. First, they ask the Benjaminites to give up the guilty men. The Benjaminites stubbornly determine to defend their own. A three-day battle ensues. For two days the Benjaminites prevail. On the third day, however, the Israelites divide their forces. As they had done at Ai long ago (Joshua 8), one force feigns retreat to draw the enemy out of the city. Then a second, hidden force sets fire to the city and attacks the enemy from behind. The defeated Benjaminites flee northeastward to the cave-pocked cliffs at Rimmon.

The story of this mini-war may combine two or more versions. Verses 37-44 in particular seem to be a separate, older account.

The extent of Israel's territory in David's time was from *Dan to Beersheba.*

Mizpah is the scene of an ancient shrine near Gibeah. This town is not to be confused with the Mizpah located east of the Jordan.

Four hundred thousand is a large army. Numbers in this story should probably not be taken literally.

The Israelites cast lots to see which tribe would go first into battle.

The extended battle serves to heighten suspense. The two defeats may also serve to weed out Israel's forces so that God, not a superior military force, might receive credit for the final victory.

Being *lefthanded* may have been a special peculiarity among Benjaminites. Ehud (Judges 3:15) was left-handed. First Chronicles 12:2 also speaks of Benjaminites using both right and left hands.

Bethel is a city north of Gibeah on the boundary between Ephraim and Benjamin. Bethel was the scene of an important shrine. The ark (container) of the covenant was normally kept at Shiloh. However, in this story the sacred object is at Bethel.

Inquire of God means to ask God's guidance. Israel does not do so before deciding on revenge. The people do seek some advice before entering battle, however. Note that God only answers the questions the people ask. God does not promise victory until the third day.

At the book's end, as in Chapter 1, Judah is the first to go into battle. It is possible that the writer included this detail for literary balance.

The location of *Baal-tamar* is unknown.

The eastern hills are called the *wilderness*.

Geba is a town on the way to Rimmon.

Nohah is a site named for one of the clans of Benjamin. Its location is unknown.

Rimmon is a limestone outcrop dotted with caves three to four miles east of Bethel.

The exact location of *Gidom* is unknown.

Making Peace Again (21:1-25)

This conclusion to the story (and the book) focuses on Israel's resourcefulness and unity despite internal strife.

The Israelites now have their revenge. Justice has been done. But what a price has been paid! Too late the Israelites realize that they have all but destroyed one of their own twelve tribes. The war has not only killed many men, but has left almost no Benjaminite women with whom the surviving soldiers could mate and rebuild the tribe. Worse yet, the other tribes had rashly vowed not to give their daughters in marriage to Benjaminites. Now the storyteller really has his listeners on cliff's edge!

But the resourceful Israelites do find a way out. The tribes had taken another sacred vow. That was to punish any group that did not join in the war. There is one city that did not participate: Jabesh-gilead. (This city had some previous marital ties with Benjamin.) The Israelites promptly attack Jabesh-gilead and kill everyone except the town's 400 young girls. These girls they turn over to the Benjaminites as a gesture of peace.

Still, 400 girls are not enough. So the Israelites devise another plan. Let the Benjaminites steal more wives at the Shiloh festival. The Benjaminites do so, the fathers of Shiloh do not break their vow by giving their daughters to Benjaminites, and the rift between the tribes is healed. No one apparently cares about the girls or about the innocent women and children killed at Jabesh-gilead. They are not the focal point of the story. The maintenance of justice and unity in faithfulness to God is the goal, and listeners can heave a sigh of relief when Israel finally achieves that goal.

The story and the whole Book of Judges end with the statement that *there was no king in Israel.* . . . This statement sums up the political reality of the judges period. It may also suggest that tragic strife like the Benjaminite war is what happens when there is neither earthly king nor careful following of Israel's divine king. Yet despite Israel's folly, that divine king has made everything come out right.

To ancient Hebrews a sacred vow had great power. If broken, the vow would bring a terrible curse or even death upon the offender. Thus, the Israelites could not consider breaking their vows under any circumstances.

Jabesh-gilead is a city east of the Jordan in the territory of Gilead.

Shiloh is a city in Ephraim north of Bethel. Shiloh was the site of a major Israelite temple.

§ § § § § § §

The Message of Judges 19–21

The writer gives no explicit interpretation to this story. Rather, the story itself shows a problem and points to a solution. The problem is how to provide justice and still maintain unity within the people of God. Israel's rather fumbling answer here was to provide justice, then find a way to heal the breach made in the process. Punish, then forgive and aid in recovery was their solution. Through all this, even though the tribes were disorganized and leaderless, they received support from their true king, God.

This message was especially important for Israel in the time of the Exile. Leaderless and broken, angry with each other and throwing blame right and left, the people needed to know that God could heal and unite their tribes once more.

Today, in our families and in our world, we face the double need to enforce right behavior while maintaining unity. We hope to find less brutal methods than Israel did for accomplishing this. Nevertheless, as we walk that tightrope between righteous indignation and healing forgiveness, we can rest assured of God's aid and support. God, in infinite power, can mend the breaks in our fractured world.

§ § § § § § §

Introduction to Ruth

Introduction to the Book of Ruth

The Book of Ruth is a historical short story. It is a love story of the conventional man-woman kind. But it is also a love story in a broader sense. This Old Testament book is a story of many good people who love and care for each other. And, beneath it all, this is a love story about God.

In Ruth, love and concern are everywhere. There is not an unkind person or a villain in the piece. There are only ordinary people showing love to family members and, beyond the family, to strangers. In this superb tale we meet unforgettable characters like Naomi, a grieving widow who looks after the interests of her daughters-in-law; Ruth, who leaves home and risks her safety to care for Naomi; and Boaz, who shows kindness to the foreigner, Ruth, and eventually marries her. Behind the scenes, guiding and protecting, we see a God whose love is stronger and broader than many humans may have suspected.

Purpose and Date

Ruth is intended to be both entertaining and instructive. One of the book's major purposes is to show that God wants people to live in self-giving love. But the author apparently had another, more specific, purpose: to deal with the problem of how Israel should relate to foreigners. Over and over the author reminds us that Ruth is from Moab, that she is a foreigner. Yet she and the other characters treat each other with love. In that light Ruth is a love story with wide social significance—a story of love between nations and groups, between people with differences who share the same parent-child relationship with God.

This second purpose probably arose from the historical situation in which the author lived. Both the language and content suggest that the story as it now stands comes from 450–250 B.C. This was a time after the Exile when Nehemiah and others were trying very hard to preserve Israel's unity and purity by limiting the people's relationships with outsiders. They strictly enforced the traditional rule forbidding intermarriage with foreigners (Nehemiah 10:28-31). They emphasized the law in Deuteronomy 23:3 that forbids foreigners from fully entering the Israelite community. Some saw foreigners as evil, inferior, or both. To many, God seemed to be God of Israel alone. Ruth's author opposed this exclusivism. But instead of writing a diatribe, he wrote a brilliantly gentle story—a story in which a loving Moabite woman marries an Israelite and eventually becomes the ancestress of Israel's greatest king.

The story itself may be a very old one. Its cultural details accurately reflect the Judges period. It contains many ancient words as well. So it seems likely that the author has taken a beloved old story and used it to make an effective point about a situation in his own time.

While most commentators agree on the book's purpose, a few do not place the author in the post-exilic time period. Some scholars argue that much of the language could come from the monarchic period, and that concern for inclusiveness could have arisen before the Exile. If this were the case, Ruth's date of composition could be set at the time of Jehoshaphat's reform in the second quarter of the ninth century B.C. However, these arguments do not seem compelling. Instead, the exilic setting still seems the more likely one.

Theology

God, in the Book of Ruth, is a God who actively cares for people. However, God works in the shadows. Occasionally God's presence is noted directly. More often, though, we hear of God through the blessings and prayers of the story's characters.

The author assumes that God is behind the good things that happen—the famine's end, the "luck" that brings Ruth to Boaz's field, and so forth. We are led to feel that God is working toward good even when evil seems dominant.

In this story God acts most often through people. They are ordinary people in ordinary circumstances. Yet they are good people, good as God is good. They live in imitation of God and, in so doing, fulfill the plans of God.

The happy ending makes one final theological point: that God will reward righteous, godly living. This is no rigid legalism, however. The author suggests that happiness will eventually come to those who love and give. The greatest happiness comes to those who love and give beyond what is legally required.

The Author

We know nothing about the author of Ruth except what we can guess from the story he wrote. We assume that he lived after the Exile and opposed the exclusiveness of that period. We can see that he preferred a subtle but effective approach, rather than direct confrontation, to make his point. He was surely a person of great sensitivity.

He was also one of the world's greatest storytellers. Ruth contains scarcely a wasted word. The plot is clear and concise. The writer has spiced his story with small but significant human details and peopled it with skillfully drawn characters. He even takes care to use archaic language in the older people's dialogue. Suspense builds steadily toward the final resolution. Then our

128

author neatly ties the story up with an all-around happy ending. This is the work of a real master!

Place in the Canon

Ruth was not originally part of the great Deuteronomic history that encompasses most of Deuteronomy through Second Kings. In the Hebrew Bible Ruth appears in the third section, among the Writings. Greek and Latin versions placed Ruth after Judges, probably because the story is set in the Judges period. Modern Bibles retain this later positioning.

Today, Jewish people read the Book of Ruth during the feast of Weeks, an ancient celebration of the grain harvest.

Ruth 1–2

Introduction to These Chapters

Ruth's author moves quickly and directly into his story. In just five verses he sets the scene, introduces two or three main characters, and sets up the problem. In the remaining verses, he shows us more about the characters' personalities, leads us to identify with them, moves the plot along, and begins to hint at the possibility of a happy ending.

An outline of this section would include:

 I. Moab (1:1-18)
 II. Bethlehem (1:19-22)
 III. Gleaning (2:1-23)

Moab (1:1-18)

The story begins with a series of tragedies. First, there is a famine in Bethlehem. To find food, an Israelite family must move to the land of Moab. There the father dies, leaving his wife and two sons. The sons marry, but soon they, too, die. That leaves three widows with no means of support. The two younger women could return to their families. Naomi, however, can only hope for help from distant relatives back in Bethlehem. As she prepares for the long, lonely journey home, Naomi urges her daughters-in-law to return to their parents. She prays, too, that the girls may find new husbands. Reluctantly, one young woman departs. Ruth, however, insists on going with Naomi. She is willing to leave her own family and nation to care for her aging mother-in-law. She knows that, in a foreign land, she will have few rights or protections and that her chances for remarriage are almost nil. She risks a life of loneliness and poverty to offer the gift of love.

The story is set rather vaguely in the Judges period (around 1200–1050 B.C.). This opening phrase might be likened to "A long time ago" or "Once upon a time."

Bethlehem means *house of bread*. The area was one of the richest grain producers in Israel. Famine there would be serious indeed.

Moab was a land on the southeastern side of the Dead Sea.

Elimelech means *God is King* or *the king is my God*.

Naomi means *delight, my joy,* or *sweet*.

Mahlon means *weakening*.

Chilion means *pining*.

The *Ephrathites* were a family group who lived in the settlement of Ephrathah, a section of Bethlehem.

The meaning of *Orpah* is uncertain. It probably is related to the word for cloud. If so, it would make a fine contrast with Ruth. Orpah is a cloud, but Ruth is a downpour.

Ruth means *water abundantly*. Ruth's kindness will make a dry and barren life bloom again.

Naomi has lost a great deal. She is *bereft*; alone with no means of support and no children. This last would be especially troubling. Ancient Hebrews did not believe in personal life after death. One's earthly life could continue, however, as it passed on into succeeding generations.

The LORD had visited his people (verse 6): This is one of the few spots where Ruth's author shows God acting directly in the story's events.

Return to Judah (verse 7): The wording means *set out on the road to Judah*. At this point Ruth and Orpah are merely accompanying Naomi for a short way.

If Mahlon and Chilion had had brothers, these brothers

would have been required to marry Ruth and Orpah, support them, and have sons by them in their dead brothers' names. But there are no more brothers. Naomi is past child-bearing age and has no husband. Even if she should somehow have new sons, it would be many years before they could grow up and marry the young widows. Staying with Naomi is not a logical solution to Ruth's and Orpah's problems.

In her grief, Naomi accuses God of making her suffer. Much Old Testament thought assumes that God is directly responsible for everything that happens.

Orpah kissed her mother-in-law good-bye. We sense that Orpah, too, loves Naomi. She does not wrong or reject Naomi. She goes back home out of common sense, obedience, or both.

Ruth's well-known vow (verses 16-17) ends the women's discussion. To break the vow would call down God's wrath. Naomi can no longer ask Ruth to change her mind.

Note that, in adopting a new land, Ruth also adopts the God of that land. The author accepts Ruth's right to do this. In fact, throughout the story he presents Ruth as an ironic model of the true Israelite, a person living in godly kindness and responsibility.

Bethlehem (1:19-22)

Ruth and Naomi reach Bethlehem. The townspeople gather around to greet their old neighbor. Naomi explains what has happened and cries out in bitterness against God for all her suffering.

The author neatly brings this section to a close by noting that the women arrive during barley harvest. This subtly brings up the problem of food and sets the stage for the next episode.

The people *stirred,* or *hummed* like a swarm of bees.

Mara means *bitter,* in contrast with Naomi's given name, which means *sweet* or *joy.*

The term *Moabitess* or the word *foreigner* is used many times to emphasize Ruth's origins.

The *barley harvest* usually takes place in late April.

Gleaning (2:1-23)

The women need food, so Ruth goes to glean. She begins working in a field that belongs to Boaz, a relative of Elimelech's. Boaz welcomes Ruth, gives her permission to glean, sees that she has food, water, and protection, and expresses appreciation for her kindness to Naomi. He even quietly instructs his field hands to leave some extra grain for Ruth to find. Boaz is obviously a kind, thoughtful person. We may even suspect that he is attracted to Ruth.

Ruth, for her part, puts in a hard day's work, takes home a good deal of grain, and even shares some of her luncheon leftovers with Naomi. By such detail the writer methodically builds up his picture of Ruth's goodness.

The meaning of *Boaz* is obscure. It may be *in him is strength*.

To *glean* is to pick up produce dropped in the harvest field. In Israel the poor had the right to glean, but that right did not extend to foreigners. Boaz offers Ruth kindness that is beyond what the law requires.

Was it really "luck" that brought Ruth to Boaz's field, or did God lead her there?

The use of the term *my daughter* suggests two things about Boaz: his age (he is much older than Ruth), and his gentle, fatherly concern for her.

Ruth risks sexual harassment or worse out in the fields alone, so she is instructed to *keep close to my maidens*.

Drink what the young men have drawn (verse 9): The water would have to be carried to the field from the town well. Because of the extra work involved, Ruth needs permission to drink.

The quantity of an *ephah* is uncertain and may have changed over the centuries. Estimates range from two-thirds of a bushel to 29 pounds to 47.5 pounds. At any rate, it was apparently a good day's gleaning.

Naomi senses a possible solution to their problem and thanks God.

Boaz is related to Elimelech. This relationship may mean that Boaz has some legal rights or obligations to Naomi. In Chapter 3 we will see that this legal situation provides the eventual solution to Ruth's and Naomi's problem.

The *wheat harvest* is in early June.

§ § § § § § §

The Message of Ruth 1–2

The message of these chapters is tied in with the message of the entire story. One part of that message is that righteous living—righteousness beyond the ordinary—brings happiness. Here we see the first steps in that process. Ruth has cared for Naomi. Now, in her need, Ruth has come to the field of an extraordinarily kind man. Moreover, this is a man in whom Naomi sees the possibility for more permanent help.

We also see here the beginnings of another message. Repeatedly the author reminds us that Ruth is a foreigner, and repeatedly we are shown that she is an unusually good person. Boaz, an obviously upright man, treats her with special kindness. Thus we learn that foreigners are not vile creatures to be avoided, but human beings with whom we can give and receive love.

These messages speak, not just to the past, but to our lives today. On a personal level, Ruth challenges us to live lives that go beyond the mediocrity of niceness. Through his story the author reminds us that real goodness is worth striving for. On both the personal and wider social levels, we who still live admist racial prejudice and international suspicion need Ruth's second message. We need Ruth's reminder that surface differences do not negate our common humanity nor our capacity to share love.

§ § § § § § §

PART EIGHTEEN Ruth 3–4

Introduction to These Chapters

Now tension builds as the story moves through a series of hurdles to what listeners hope will be a happy ending. Naomi and Ruth take a large, but calculated risk; Boaz, though willing to help the women, must get by a legal obstacle. For a time, that legality nearly ruins the hoped-for solution. But, in the end, goodness triumphs, and "they all live happily ever after." Thus the writer skillfully develops his story to climax and resolution.

Someone, either the basic author or a later editor, has added a genealogy to the happy ending. The list follows Ruth's descendants down to King David. This information is not necessary to the plot but serves to underline the author's message that God accepts foreigners and that Israel should do so too. After all, if David had a Moabite great-grandmother, can Moabites be all that bad?

These chapters can be divided into three parts:
I. Naomi's Plan (3:1-18)
II. A Slight Hitch (4:1-12)
III. Conclusion (4:13-22)

Naomi's Plan (3:1-18)

Naomi outlines to Ruth a rather daring plan. Ruth is to fix herself up prettily, go to Boaz at night, and ask for his protection as a kinsman. The situation is a seductive one and not without dangers. Naomi is counting very heavily on Boaz's goodness.

Ruth approaches Boaz as Naomi has instructed. Boaz does prove to be as good a man as Naomi had hoped. He protects Ruth and agrees to help the women. He warns, however, that there is a stumbling block. Another man is a nearer relative than he. This other man has first right and obligation in the matter. Boaz must somehow get this man to forfeit his position.

Ruth returns home early in the morning when she can walk safely. At this time of the morning, however, it is still dark enough to protect both her own and Boaz's reputations. Boaz sends a gift for Naomi as a kindness and a sign of goodwill.

The author's flair for human detail is especially apparent in these verses. Naomi's plan is psychologically perfect. It appeals to the attraction we suspect Boaz feels for Ruth while also appealing, Naomi hopes, to his protective instinct. How can a good man refuse an attractive woman who obviously needs help, especially if he is already halfway in love with her?

Through the plan and its execution the author heightens the story's tension. Listeners know that Ruth is taking a big chance, and they hope that Boaz will be worthy of Naomi's trust. Then, while we are still sighing with relief that Ruth is all right, we learn of the nearer-kinsman obstacle. Naomi's admonition to "wait and see" is the perfect note for the author to close this chapter and draw listeners into the next. This writer definitely knows how to keep his audience on the edges of their seats!

Ancient Israelites separated the chaff from the grain by forking the grain up into a breeze and letting the wind blow the chaff away. Early evening was usually the best time for this. Boaz would have to stay through the night, however, to guard his grain from theft.

Uncover his feet (verse 4): This is a "loaded" expression. The author may have used it intentionally, knowing that its ambiguity would increase the story's tension. *Feet* (or in some translations *legs*) is often used in the Old Testament as a euphemism for genital organs. It also can mean simply feet. How much does Naomi mean for Ruth to uncover? We learn shortly that Naomi does mean feet literally. Ruth is to carry out a symbolic act as part of her request for help. But the phrase's double meaning reminds listeners that this situation is fraught with temptation. Despite that temptation, these two good people will choose the best of behaviors.

In saying, *Spread your skirt*, Ruth is asking for Boaz's protection. The word *skirt* is translated in 2:12 as God's *wings*, the place where one finds shelter. Here it refers to a corner of Boaz's garment.

Boaz is delighted that Ruth has come to him. He recognizes that the kinsman's duty involves marrying her, and he has loved her for some time. He is much older than she, however, and perhaps has feared that she would want a younger husband. How thrilled he is to learn that she does not! Now he who was alone will also know the joy of marriage.

The word for *lie down* is the word for *lodge*. It carries no sexual connotations. By using this word, the writer thus reassures us that, despite the circumstances, Boaz will act honorably.

A Slight Hitch (4:1-12)

Next morning Boaz begins legal action. To work things properly he must somehow deal with the nearer kinsman. Boaz assembles the town elders. He announces the sale of Naomi's land. The nearer kinsman has the first right and obligation for the land and for Naomi's care. The man, seeing his duty, agrees. But Boaz reminds him that the deal also includes Ruth. The man reconsiders. He has a family of his own. He would have to support Ruth and Naomi and have a son by Ruth. That son would inherit the land. Investing in this land would not do the man's own children any good. The whole package is going to be very expensive for him with little compensation in return. Boaz seems interested, so the man offers to relinquish his rights. Boaz gladly accepts them.

The *gate* was the place where the elders met to settle legal questions and other town affairs.

The nearer kinsman remains unnamed. Perhaps the author is saying that this man's personality is not important to the story; only his status is. Did he come by chance? Had Boaz alerted him to come? Had God guided him there? The author does not say.

Ten men is the number needed for a marriage benediction. Boaz wants to be ready.

When Boaz mentions a *parcel of land,* it is the first time we hear of any land being involved. Ruth or Naomi may have spoken of it to Boaz, but the writer has not told us so. It is possible that Boaz himself remembered a piece of land and devised his plan around it.

The man would not be literally *buying Ruth* as a slave. Ruth does, however, go with the land as part of the kinsman's obligation.

Rachel and Leah were Jacob's wives, the mothers of all Israel.

All children after the first son would be credited to Boaz. He who had no son will now have many. Boaz's life will pass to another generation.

Conclusion (4:13-22)

Ruth and Boaz marry. They have a son who is credited to Mahlon. He is thus a grandson for Naomi. This child will eventually become the grandfather of Israel's greatest king, David.

Naomi again has a family and the joy of children. What's more she has a "descendant" to carry on her life and that of Elimelech.

The genealogy of verses 18-22 may be a later addition to the story. It emphasizes the fact that even David carried Moabite blood. Besides underlining acceptance of foreigners, this reference to David might have been an important factor in the book's inclusion among the sacred writings.

Note that the genealogy goes through Boaz rather than Mahlon. This may be a slip on the part of the genealogy writer or it may indicate some variations in traditions about David.

§ § § § § § §

The Message of Ruth 3–4

The book's double message carries through to its conclusion. Here, as in earlier chapters, we see that (1) goodness brings eventual happiness, and (2) God accepts other peoples and wants Israel to do the same. Underneath everything we see the hand of God caring for the people, leading them toward joy.

It is easy for modern Christians to be drawn into the selfishness, the mediocrity, the prejudice, and the cynicism of the world around us. A book like Ruth reminds us again that more-than-conventional goodness is worthwhile, that prejudice and exclusiveness are not God's ways, and that God really does care and work toward our happiness. We need that reminder. Thank God for giving it to us in this exquisite little story!

§ § § § § § §

Glossary of Terms

Abdon: A judge from Ephraim. He provided wise administration in time of peace.

Abimelech: A son of Gideon. Abimelech killed his brothers and set himself up as king of Shechem.

Achan: A man from the tribe of Judah who stole booty devoted to God. Achan's sin caused Joshua's army to lose in its first attempt to capture Ai.

Achor: A valley on the northern border of Judah. In this valley Joshua executed Achan for stealing booty from the defeated city of Jericho.

Achsah: The daughter of Caleb and wife of Othniel. Achsah asked for and received rights to a spring for Othniel's land in the Negeb.

Adonizedek: King of Jerusalem. Adonizedek led four other kings in opposing Joshua's conquest of Palestine. Joshua killed him at Makkedah.

Ai: "The ruin," a city near Bethel.

Amalekites: A nomadic tribe that ranged over the Palestine area.

Ammonites: A non-Israelite tribe living in the territory east of the Jordan.

Amorites: A non-Israelite tribe. Some Amorites lived in the area claimed by Judah; others lived east of the Jordan in Bashan and Heshbon.

Anakim: A tribe, described as giants, that inhabited Canaan before the Israelite conquest. Anakim are usually connected with southern sites.

Angel: A messenger of God.

Arabah: The Jordan Valley. The Arabah may also include the Dead Sea and the area from the Dead Sea to the Gulf of Aqabah.

Ark of the Covenant: Sacred box holding the law. The ark represented God's powerful presence among the people.

Asher: One of the twelve tribes of Israel. Asher settled in the north near the seacoast.

Asherah: A Semitic goddess or a cult object related to her worship. The King James Version mistranslates the term as "grove."

Ashkelon: A Philistine city located on the Mediterranean seacoast.

Astarte/Ashtoreth (pl. Ashtaroth): A Canaanite goddess used in worship rituals.

Azekah: A city in southern Palestine about fifteen miles northwest of Hebron. Here a rain of hailstones helped Joshua defeat Adonizedek's forces.

Baal: A Canaanite god.

Ban: A decree requiring absolute destruction of everything in a conquered city.

Barak: A judge who, with Deborah, led Israel in defeating Sisera.

Bashan: Amorite territory east of the Jordan and well to the north.

Benjamin: One of the twelve tribes of Israel. Benjamin's territory was in southern Palestine in the territory north of the Dead Sea.

Bethel: A city in central Palestine. Early in the Judges period the ark of the covenant was at Bethel.

Bethlehem: (1) A city south of Jerusalem, original home of Micah's Levite, of the Ephraimite Levite's concubine, and of Naomi and Boaz. (2) A town the same name to the north, in Zebulun.

Beth-millo: A fortress at Shechem.

Boaz: Ruth's protector and second husband.

Caleb: One of the spies who entered Canaan before the Israelite conquest. In the land division he received the city of Hebron.

Canaan: Palestine west of the Jordan extending into the coast of Syria.

Canaanites: Non-Israelites who inhabited Palestine.

Chemosh: A Moabite god.

Chilion: Noami's son, Orpah's husband.

Chinnereth, Chinneroth: Sea of Galilee.

Circumcise: To remove the foreskin from the male genital organ. In Israel, circumcision was a sign of dedication to God and membership in God's people.

Conquest: The period (thirteenth century B.C.) when Israel entered Palestine and took possession of the land.

Covenant: A sacred agreement.

Cubit: About eighteen inches.

Cushan-rishathaim: King of Aram-naharaim, the first oppressor in the Book of Judges. He was defeated by the Israelite judge Othniel.

D: Any biblical writer or editor of the Deuteronomic school. D writers were especially active around the time of King Josiah (7th century B.C.) and after the Exile (587–538 B.C.). Joshua and Judges are D works.

Dagon: A Philistine god.

Dan: One of the twelve tribes of Israel. Dan first settled in the southern plains, then moved to the far north.

Debir: A city in southern Palestine; also, the king of Eglon who joined in a coalition opposing Joshua.

Deborah: A judge who united several tribes of Israel to defeat their Canaanite oppressors.

Delilah: Philistine woman who led Samson into slavery.

Deuteronomic: Referring to a literary group and its common theological outlook. The Deuteronomists produced a lengthy history of Israel, including the books of Deuteronomy, Joshua, and Judges.

Ebal: A mountain near Shechem situated opposite Mount Gerizim.

Eglon: A city in southern Palestine whose king opposed Joshua; also, the Moabite king whom Ehud killed.

Ehud: A Benjaminite hero who stabbed the oppressive Moabite king, Eglon.

Eleazar: A priest at the time of Joshua.

Elimelech: Naomi's husband.

Elon: A minor judge from Zebulun.

Ephah: A unit of measure whose value is now uncertain. Various estimates give it 2/3 bushel, 29 pounds, and 47.5 pounds.

Ephod: A priestly garment.

Ephraim: Son of Joseph and one of the twelve tribes of Israel. When Joshua divided the land, the priestly tribe of Levi received no portion, but Joseph received two, one for Ephraim and one for Manasseh. Thus there were still twelve territorial divisions. Ephraim's land was in the hill country of central Palestine.

Exile: Period from the Fall of Jerusalem (587 B.C.) to the Jews' release (538 B.C.). During this time many of Israel's people lived as captives in Babylon.

Exodus: The escape of Moses and the Hebrews from oppression in Egypt.

Gaal: The man who turned the people of the city of Shechem against Abimelech.

Gad: One of the twelve tribes. Gad settled in the territory east of the Jordan.

Gate: Entrance to a walled city and public gathering place. In ancient Israel, the elders sat at the city gate to carry out legal activities.

Gaza: A Philistine city near the southern coast.

Gerizim: A mountain near Shechem situated opposite Mount Ebal.

Gezer: A city in the Palestinian plain.

Gibeah: The inhospitable Benjaminite city whose men killed a traveling Levite's concubine and provoked a war.

Gibeon: A city six miles northwest of Jerusalem whose people made a treaty with Joshua.

Gideon: Judge from Manasseh who rid Israel of Midianite oppression. He is known for panicking the enemy army with sudden torchlight, noise, and victory shouts.

Gilead: A large area east of the Jordan.

Gilgal: A city close to the Jordan near Jericho. Gilgal was Israel's main base during the conquest.

Girgashites: A non-Israelite tribe living in Palestine.

Glean: To pick up leftover produce in a harvest field.

Great Sea: The Mediterranean.

Hazor: A Canaanite city in the north whose king opposed Joshua. In Deborah's time, Hazor was a center of Canaanite oppression.

Hebron: A city nineteen miles south of Jerusalem. The Anakim occupied Hebron until Caleb captured it.

Hittites: A people from the north who maintained a vast Middle-eastern empire before the time of Israel's conquest of Palestine.

Hivites: A people living in Canaan before the Israelite conquest. The name is sometimes interchanged with *Horites*.

Hoham: King of Hebron who opposed Joshua.

Horites: Hurrians dwelling in Palestine, sometimes called *Hivites*.

Ibzan: A minor judge from the border between Asher and Zebulun. He administered his area in time of peace.

Jabesh-gilead: A city east of the Jordan which did not participate in the Benjaminite war. As punishment, its people were killed except for 400 virgins who were given to the surviving Benjaminites.

Jabin: King of Hazor who opposed Joshua; also one of the oppressors against whom Deborah revolted.

Jael: Woman who murdered Sisera as he fled from Deborah and Barak's troops.

Jair: Minor judge from Gilead who administered his territory in peacetime.

Japhia: King of Lachish who joined in a coalition to oppose Joshua.

Jarmuth: A city in Judah which opposed Joshua's invasion.

Jashar, Book of: An ancient book of poetry containing Joshua's address to the sun and moon.

Jebusites: Canaanite tribe that occupied the city of Jebus (Jerusalem).

Jephthah: Judge from Gilead who rid Israel of invading Ammonites and sacrificed his daughter to fulfill a vow.

Jephunneh: Caleb's father.

Jericho: A city near the west bank of the Jordan, sometimes called the "city of palms." Jericho was the first city Joshua captured.

Jerubaal: Another name for Gideon.

Jezreel: A town in Issachar at the foot of Mount Gilboa; a plain and a valley near the town.

JOSHUA, JUDGES, AND RUTH

Joash: Gideon's father.

Jordan: The river that runs north and south along the mountainous spine of Palestine.

Joshua: Moses' successor, the general who led Israel in its conquest and settlement of Palestine.

Jotham: Son of Gideon who survived Abimelech's slaughter and spoke out against Abimelech's coronation as king of Shechem.

Judah: One of the twelve tribes of Israel. Judah settled in the south of Palestine.

Judges: (1) Charismatic persons who gave Israel military and administrative leadership before Israel had a king; (2) the time when the judges ruled (approximately 1200–1050 B.C.); (3) the biblical book that tells the stories of the judges.

Kadesh-barnea: A town south of Israel where the Hebrews stayed after leaving Mount Sinai.

Kedesh: Barak's home in eastern Galilee. Deborah and Barak mustered their troops there.

Kenaz: An Edomite clan chief, ancestor of the Kenizites; Othniel's father.

Kenites: Semi-nomadic people living in the territory south of Palestine.

Kenizites: An Edomite tribe living in southern Judah and the Negeb. Caleb and Othniel were Kenizites.

Kinsman: A relative. The nearest kinsman had the first right to purchase a relative's land. He also had certain obligations toward his relative's widow.

Kiriath-arba: Ancient name for Debir.

Kishon: A stream running from the Palestinian hills to the sea.

Lachish: A city in Judah midway between Jerusalem and Gaza.

Laish: Canaanite city in northern Palestine later known as Dan.

Lebanon: A mountain range located in the area to the north of Palestine.

Lehi: "The jawbone," a place between Zorah and Timnah where Samson fought the Philistines.

Levi: One of the tribes of Israel. The men of Levi were set aside to serve as priests. In the land division, Levi did not receive a territorial inheritance. Instead the Levites were assigned certain cities spread throughout Palestine.

Levite: A priest, a member of the tribe of Levi.

Machir: A clan of Manasseh. Some texts locate Machir east of the Jordan, others to the west.

Madon: A Canaanite town in Galilee that joined Jabin's confederation against Joshua.

Mahaneh-dan: Camp of Dan, a place located to the west of Kiriath-jearim.

Mahlon: Naomi's son, Ruth's first husband.

Makkedah: A Canaanite city near which Joshua trapped five kings in a cave.

Manasseh: Son of Joseph and one of the twelve tribes of Israel. Manasseh claimed territory on both sides of the Jordan.

Megiddo: A city overlooking the Valley of Jezreel in central Palestine.

Merom: A stream in Upper Galilee.

Mesopotamia: The area between the Tigris and Euphrates rivers far to the east of Palestine.

Micah: An Ephraimite from whom the Danites took religious objects and a priest.

Midianites: A nomadic tribe living to the south and east of Palestine.

Mizpah: A town in Benjamin; a town in Gilead; a town in Judah; a town in Moab; a valley located in the territory to the north of Palestine.

Moab: A land east of the Dead Sea. Israel camped in Moab before entering the Promised Land. Ruth was originally from Moab.

Naomi: Ruth's mother-in-law.

Naphtali: One of the twelve tribes of Israel. Naphtali settled on the west side of the Jordan in Galilee.

Nazirite: A person specially dedicated to God. The period of dedication could be temporary or life-long. Some Nazirites were designated by God; others chose to dedicate themselves. Later Nazirites distinguished themselves by abstaining from alcohol, by not cutting their hair, and by avoiding contact with the dead. However, earlier accounts do not include the third restriction.

Negeb: An arid area on the southern edge of Palestine.

Ophrah: Gideon's hometown in Manasseh.

Orpah: Naomi's daughter-in-law. After her husband died, Orpah chose to return to her family while Ruth vowed to remain forever with Naomi.

Othniel: The first deliverer listed in the Book of Judges. Othniel was an Edomite who became a part of the Israelite tribe of Judah. A kinsman of Caleb, Othniel captured Debir during the conquest and married Caleb's daughter. Later he rid Israel of the oppressor Cushan-rishathaim.

Penuel: A city on the east side of the Jordan. Gideon killed its inhabitants for refusing to help him.

Peor: A mountain in Moab.

Perizzites: Non-Israelites living in Canaan.

Philistines: Canaanite people who lived along the southern coast of the Mediterranean. During the Judges period they sometimes pushed inland, squeezing the Israelite tribes settled there.

Phinehas: The priest who settled the problem of an altar built by the eastern tribes.

Piram: King of Jarmuth who opposed Joshua's invasion.

Pisgah: A mountain in Moab across the Jordan from Jericho.

Rahab: A prostitute who sheltered the spies Joshua sent to Jericho.

Rephaim: Early inhabitants of Palestine described as giants; also a valley near Jerusalem.

Reuben: One of the twelve tribes of Israel. Reuben occupied land east of the Jordan.

Ruth: (1) A four-chapter short story which follows the Book of Judges; (2) the main figure in that story, a Moabite woman whose love and loyalty to her Israelite mother-in-law gave her a special place in God's chosen people.

Samson: An extremely strong man whom God used to punish Israel's Philistine oppressors.

Shamgar: A judge who killed large numbers of Philistines.

Shechem: An ancient Canaanite city in Ephraim, later an important Israelite center.

Shiloh: An important Israelite worship center located in Ephraim.

Shittim: A place in the plains of Moab, Israel's last campsite before crossing the Jordan.

Sidon: A Phoenician coastal city.

Simeon: One of the twelve tribes of Israel. Simeon occupied land in the far south of Palestine.

Succoth: A city east of the Jordan which Gideon punished for failing to help him.

Taanach: A city in Manasseh, one site for the battle between Sisera and Barak.

Tabor: A mountain in the Valley of Jezreel.

Teraphim: One or more idols.

Thebez: A town near Shechem attacked by Abimelech.

Theology: Understanding of God, study or discussion about God.

Timnah: A town on the northern border of Judah, home of Samson's wife.

Timnath-heres (Timnath-serah): Joshua's city.

Tola: A minor judge from Issachar.

Transjordanian tribes: The tribes of Reuben, Gad, and half of Manasseh which settled east of the Jordan.

Urim and Thummim: Sacred lots, a way of determining the will of God.

Zebulun: One of the twelve tribes of Israel. Zebulun occupied land in north-central Palestine.

Guide to Pronunciation

Abdon: AB-dun
Abimelech: Ah-BIH-meh-lek
Abinoam: Ah-bih-NOH-um
Achan: AH-kun
Achor: Ah-CORE
Achsah: AHK-sah
Achshaph: AHK-shahf
Adonizedek: Ah-doh-nigh-ZEH-dek
Ai: EYE
Aijalon: AY-jah-lon
Amalekites: Ah-MAL-eh-kites
Anakim: Ah-nah-KEEM
Aphek: AY-fek
Arabah: AR-ah-bah
Arad: AIR-ad
Aroer: Ah-ROH-er
Asherah: AH-sheh-rah
Ashtaroth: Ash-teh-ROTHE
Astarte: Ah-START
Azekah: Ah-zeh-KAH
Baal: Bah-ALL
Barak: Bah-RAK
Bashan: Bah-SHAHN
Bethhoron: Beth-HOR-un
Bethjeshimoth: Beth-jeh-shih-MOTHE
Boaz: BO-az
Bochim: Boh-KEEM
Chemosh: Keh-MOSH

Chilion: KIL-ee-un
Chinnereth: KIH-neh-reth
Cushan-rishathaim: KOO-shan-rish-uh-THAY-im
Debir: Deh-BEER
Edrei: EH-dreh-eye
Ehud: EE-hude
Eleazar: Eh-lee-AY-zar
Elimelech: Eh-lee-MEH-lek
Elon: EE-lon
Enhakkore: En-hah-KORE
Ephah: EE-fah
Ephod: EE-fod
Ephraim: EE-frah-eem
Eshtaol: ESH-tah-ole
Gaal: Gah-ALL
Gezer: GEH-zer
Gibeah: GIH-bee-ah
Gideon: GIH-dee-un
Gilead: GIH-lee-ad
Gilgal: GIL-gal
Goiim: Goh-EEM
Harosheth-ha-goiim: Hah-roh-SHETH-hah-goh-EEM
Hinnom: Hih-NOME
Hittites: HIT-ites
Jabesh-gilead: Jah-besh-GIH-lee-ad
Jabin: JAY-bin
Jael: Jah-ELL
Jair: Jah-EER
Jashar: Jah-SHAHR
Jebus: JEH-bus
Jebusite: JEB-you-site
Jephthah: JEF-thah
Jericho: JEH-rih-koh
Jerubaal: Jeh-ROO-bah-all
Jephunneh: Jeh-FOO-neh
Jezreel: JEZ-reh-eel
Joash: JO-ash
Jokneam: Joke-NEE-um

152

Jotham: JOH-thum
Kadesh-barnea: Kah-desh-bar-NEE-uh
Kedesh: KEH-desh
Kenaz: KEH-naz
Kenites: KEH-nites
Kenizzites: KEH-nih-zites
Kiriath-arba: Kir-ee-ath-AR-buh
Kiriath-sepher: Kir-ee-ath-SAY-fer
Kishon: KEE-shon
Lachish: Lah-KEESH
Laish: Lah-EESH
Lasharon: Lah-shah-RONE
Lehi: LEE-high
Levite: LEE-vite
Libnah: LIB-nuh
Machir: Mah-KEER
Madon: Mah-DON
Mahlon: Mah-LON
Makkedah: Mah-kay-DAH
Manasseh: Muh-NASS-eh
Megiddo: Meh-GID-oh
Merom: Mare-OME
Micah: MY-cuh
Misrephoth-maim: MIZ-reh-foth-mah-EEM
Midianites: MID-ee-uh-nites
Moab: MOH-ab
Naomi: Nay-OH-mee
Naphath-dor: Nah-fath-DOR
Naphtali: Naf-TAL-lee
Negeb: NEH-geb
Orpah: OR-puh
Penuel: PEN-yoo-el
Peor: Peh-ORE
Perizzites: PER-iz-ites
Philistines: FIH-liss-teens
Pisgah: PIZ-guh
Rahab: RAY-hab
Rephaim: Reh-fah-EEM

Salecah: Sah-leh-KAH
Shechem: SHEK-um
Shiloh: SHY-low
Shimron-meron: Shim-RONE-meer-OWN
Shittim: Shih-TEEM
Succoth: SUH-cuth
Taanach: Tah-ah-NAHK
Tappuah: Tah-POO-uh
Teraphim: Teh-rah-FEEM
Thebez: THEH-bez
Thummim: THUM-im
Timnah: Tim-NAH
Timnath-serah: Tim-nath-seh-RAH
Tola: TOH-lah
Urim: YOOR-im
Zebulun: ZEB-yoo-lun

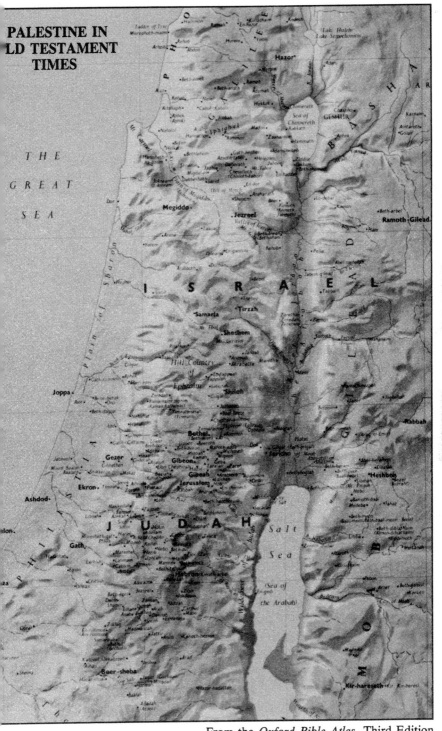

PALESTINE IN
LD TESTAMENT
TIMES

THE GREAT SEA

From the *Oxford Bible Atlas*, Third Edition

Black

R. Sangarius

P H R Y G I A
Gordion •
Gomer
(Gimarrai)
Meshech
(Mushki)

G R E E C E
R. Hermus
L Y D I A
R. Halys
Usiana •

Corinth• • Athens
Sardis •
(Sepharad)
• Maeander

J A V A N
C I L I C I A
(KHILAKKU)Kue
• Ura

Lycia
Pitusu

Rhodes

Crete
(Caphtor)
Cyprus
(Iadanna)

T h e
Arvad •

G r e a t   *S e a*
Gebal (Byblos)•
Berytus •

(The Upper Sea, the Western Sea)
Sidon•
Tyre• •Ushu
Acco •

Megiddo •
ISRAEL
Samaria •

L i b y a
Jerusalem•   AM
Gaza• JUDAH MO

Sais • Zoan
(Tanis)
Tahpanhes
Raphia

Athribis •
EDO
Sela• •Tar

Memphis •
(Noph)
•Heliopolis
(On)
•Ezion-ge
(Elath)

E G Y P T
S i n a

Hermopolis •
R.

Lycopolis •
(Siut)
N i l e

R e d

Thebes •
S e a

E T H I O P I A
•Syene

THE ANCIENT NEAR EAST
IN THE TIME OF
THE ASSYRIAN EMPIRE

Approximate extent of Assyrian domination
in the latter part of the 8th. Century
(Later, under Esarhaddon (681-669), Assyria conquered Egypt)

From the *Oxford Bible Atlas*, Third Edition